CHESS for FUN

&

CHESS for BLOOD

By

EDWARD LASKER

Illustrated by

MAXIMILIAN MOPP

DOVER PUBLICATIONS, INC.
NEW YORK

This new Dover edition, first published in 1962, is an unabridged and corrected republication of the second edition of the work first published by David McKay Company in 1942.

Standard Book Number: 486-20146-5
Library of Congress Catalog Card Number: 63-22968

Manufactured in the United States of America

Dover Publications, Inc.
180 Varick Street
New York, N. Y. 10014

THIS BOOK IS DEDICATED TO THOSE WHO
PREFER THE RAPIER TO THE BLUDGEON
AND WHO—AT LEAST IN RECREATION,
ESCAPING THE WORKADAY'S BANALITIES
—ENJOY APPLYING TO THEIR OWN
CREATIONS THEIR IMAGINATION, SKILL
AND HUMOR.

Preface

Had it not been for Chess I should never have met some of the outstanding men and women, in many walks of life, whose acquaintance has enriched my days. Among them I count some of my best friends—reason enough for me to be grateful to the game.

I asked a few of them to write to me why Chess has been their favorite game through all these years, and I do not think I could preface this book more fittingly than by printing their replies.

New York, July 15th, 1941

EDWARD LASKER.

FROM AN ADVERTISING MAN:

E. T. Gundlach, President of the Advertising Company bearing his
name, was at one time President of the City Club and Chess Champion of the University Club of Chicago. He is the author of "Old Sox
on Trumpeting" and "Facts and Fetishes in Advertising."

Dear Mr. Lasker:

*From the age of eight to this day I have been a Chess
"fan." My father played it and my mother played it a great
deal. I prefer it to all other games because it limits the element of luck and because it is a game in which strategy and
tactics bring the victory.*

*When I read your book on Chess I acquired a new point
of view. I realize now that strategy is paramount, and not tactics. It was an education in Chess and an education in life.
For, your book, besides showing the steps one must take to
reach a certain goal, showed that first of all a plan to reach
that goal must be laid out.*

*I note that you are publishing another book and I am sure
that Chess players everywhere in the United States and, in
fact, in Europe and Asia will want to know what next Edward
Lasker has to offer on this subject.*

Yours sincerely,

E. T. GUNDLACH

FROM AN ARTIST:

Everyone who has seen Maximilian Mopp's unique "Quartet" or "Symphony Concert" will have gathered that he likes to paint hands. The picture of his which is reproduced on the jacket represents a Chess variation of his predilection.

Dear Doctor Lasker:

Confound your Chess! A fat Bishop sat upon my chest all night! I tried to get him with a mammoth Tank-Rook of mine, but I could not move and suffered agonies while the Bishop captured my Rook. When I awoke I saw him lie on the edge of the board—an insignificant little wooden corpse.

Yes, that is Chess for you! It keeps your phantasy working even when the game is over. All the same, I always return to it again, like many of my artist-friends. We have to use our phantasy so much in our work that the exercise of the imagination in Chess exerts a fascination hard to resist.

I am sure Chess is of real value to all those who have to keep their wits sharpened for a struggle. It teaches the elements important in a fight—the coordinated development of the forces, their economical employment, the invention of traps and ambushes—and proves beyond doubt that defence alone never wins a battle and that victory demands initiative, foresight and perseverance.

In my home town there was a famous football player who was also a devotee of Chess. He weighed much less than any of the other boys on his team, but he saved many a game by extraordinary combinations which nobody had anticipated. The inference is obvious.

I wish the generals in this war knew how to play Chess. I know it would improve their tactics and their strategy.

Yours,

MAXIMILIAN MOPP

FROM A BUSINESSMAN:

Alfred MacArthur is President of the Central Life Insurance Company of Illinois. While he probably does not object to being referred to as the brother-in-law of Helen Hayes, he is better known to the Chess world as a patron and genial host of Chess masters visiting the "Windy City."

My dear Mr. Lasker,

I am glad to see that you are applying yourself to a book on Chess that emphasizes the potential interest of the game to a large group of people who erroneously assume that its enjoyment depends on deep study, years of practice, oceans of time, and "that kind of a mind." As a mere nibbler at the great intellectual feast set out upon the Chess table, I can testify that the game is a delightful pastime, without any of these things.

It is a mental gymnasium that benefits the weak as well as the strong, the toddling mental infant as well as the psycological Sandow like yourself. It is always there, ready to meet your mood—the fierce contest if you want it; the dilettante contemplation of a delicately balanced problem if you wish. A game lost to a friend is of no moment while a game won does give you a gentle glow once in a while. A Chess problem is better than solitaire or a cross word puzzle, the game itself a better contest than Bridge. All together, in my opinion, this is the real "sport of kings."

I have heard as criticism that the game is not social. This is, of course, nonsense. I have found nothing that promoted domestic felicity as much as studying the game of a great master, allowing my wife to hold the book and make the opponent's moves, and then fumbling around until I found the move that the book calls for. I improved my game somewhat and the charming partner of my existence passed a pleasant evening telling me I was wrong 49 times out of 50. This diver-

sion is more enjoyable than back seat driving for both parties.

Of course, there are some drawbacks in the game itself. Unlike Bridge, you have no partner on whom you can blame the loss of the game. The element of luck is entirely absent! You have no excuse or alibi. Your own deficiencies stand out in a very stark and realistic fashion, but you will win now and then and the boot is on the other foot. A game you can play by correspondence or from a wheel chair, a pastime in youth and a comfort in old age, will repay even casual attention and richly reward deeper study.

Very sincerely yours,

ALFRED MACARTHUR

FROM A LAWYER:

Huntington Cairns, Assistant General Counsel of the Treasury Department, is known to Radio audiences as the Chairman of the program "Invitation to Learning." He is the author of "Law and the Social Sciences" and "The Theory of Legal Science."

Dear Edward Lasker:

It is good to know that you are publishing a new book on Chess. Your previous volume Chess Strategy taught me much that I know about the game. Not that I ever play Chess for blood; that requires the application of a life-time. But Chess for fun—by which I suppose you mean games based on mere skill as opposed to games based on knowledge as to what the Chess masters have done—is for me in my declining years still a great source of pleasure, and, with the game of Go, my favorite relaxation.

Chess mastery, except perhaps for the phenomenally gifted, demands, I think, nothing less than the unremitting *concentration of the full energies of those who would achieve it. In this respect Chess is no different from any other occupation. It has its men of supreme genius but even they, if they would reach the superlative—to use a phrase of Justice Holmes—must give the best that is in them. The satisfactions, no doubt, are rewarding; but they can be won only by unstinting effort.*

Chess for fun is an altogether different world. It is a part of the world of play. That is to say, in accordance with the theory of play put forward by Schiller, it represents expenditure of energy in exuberant and unnecessary ways. In that realm the demonic power of Chess for blood, which makes an exhausted man of a Zuckertort at twenty-four, no longer exerts its malignant force. The amateur plays Chess for fun for the same reason that he dances and sings, shouts and capers; he is discharging an excess of vigor. Since he has nothing at stake, his play will not be marked by neurotic intensity. He may exhibit a mild interest in the games of experts, but he will hardly be connoisseur enough to detect the elements of Classicism and Romanticism which some observers have found in modern play. He will take it, in short, simply for what it is—one of the best games yet devised by the mind of men.

The best of luck for Chess for Fun and Chess for Blood.

Yours ever,

HUNTINGTON CAIRNS

FROM A MATHEMATICIAN:

> Horace C. Levinson, Ph.D., mathematician and astronomer, is Treasurer of L. Bamberger & Co. He is the author of "The Law of Gravitation in Relativity" and "Your Chance to Win."

Dear Edward:

Not long after receiving your note asking for a line or two on the subject of Chess I was forcibly reminded of it by a rather curious coincidence. A letter arrived from one of my earliest friends of the Chess board, whom I had not seen in twenty-five years. He suggested that since he had just found out that he and I were only a short distance apart, we meet again and perhaps have a friendly game of Chess.

Chess suggests so many things that it may be best to limit oneself to one. The phase of the game that perhaps has always appealed to me the most is what one might call its aesthetic content. The emotion aroused by a superlative series of moves is related to that aroused by a work of art or a beautiful mathematical theorem. There are the same elements of economy, simplicity emerging from complexity, harmony and power.

I feel that I owe a great debt to the game of Chess for helping me, during my formative years, to attain a sharper appreciation of such things. I recall (without quite believing it now) that when in high school I frequently got up an hour earlier than necessary in order to play over games from one of the books, and I have very naturally always preferred such games, from the standpoint of aesthetics, to those in which I was one of the combatants.

Yours as always,

HORACE C. LEVINSON

FROM A MUSICIAN:

Mischa Elman needs no introduction as master of the violin; but comparatively few people know of his prowess on the Chess board.

Dear Edward,

I think one reason why Chess appeals so much to musicians is that playing it is like composing; and to the pleasure of creating your own harmonies there is added the excitement of a struggle.

To me it has always seemed that Chess is a game closely related to life itself. It teaches you how to coordinate reason with instinct. It teaches you to be responsible for your own mistakes. It teaches you not to underestimate the other fellow at any time, if you wish to survive. It teaches you to accept defeat with a smile and to realize that a Pawn cannot always become a Queen, and that not everybody can become a Lasker.

With best greetings,

MISCHA ELMAN

FROM A PHILOSOPHER:

Ernst Cassirer, Visiting Professor of Philosophy at Yale, holds honorary degrees from the Universities of Glasgow and Goeteborg. Among the many books he has written best known are "Philosophy of Symbolic Form" and "Substance and Function."

Dear Edward Lasker:

You ask me a difficult question; and if you expect an answer from the philosopher rather than from the old friend, I am afraid I have to disappoint you.

"Rerum cognoscere causas"—to know and to understand the reasons of things, according to Lucretius, is the principal

task of philosophy. But a philosopher is rarely inclined to analyze his feelings and predilections. Like all others, he is in the habit of taking his personal inclinations for granted. For this reason I had really never asked myself why of all the games in the world I liked Chess best. When, after receiving your letter, I considered this question, the answer seemed at first simple and obvious. Does not Chess satisfy the demands of our intellect in the highest degree? Nothing is left to chance; the consequences of every move obey definite rules; and thus reason and logic triumph.

But this explanation, flattering as it may be, unfortunately does not apply in my case, though it may hold good in the case of Chess masters. It seems paradoxical, but the reasons for my love of Chess are not only different from but probably even opposed to those of a Chess master.

The master has to solve a definite problem and concentrates on it with the greatest thoroughness and penetration. But all this would be lost effort for a poor amateur like me. I know very well that even after having done my best to find out the strongest move, I cannot rely upon my reasoning. I have to confide in that mysterious and unfathomable power that we may call the "Fate of Chess." Sometimes that goddess smiles upon me graciously, and sometimes she works against me.

However, I feel by no means discouraged by the uncertainty which threatens me on every move. On the contrary, I find in that uncertainty a particular charm—the charm of the "imprévu," which according to Stendhal is one of the greatest.

I think it is just this opposition to his usual way of thinking and feeling which makes a game of Chess so enjoyable to a scientist and a philosopher. Both of them would undoubtedly be much ashamed if in their own fields of investigation they made such glaring mistakes as they constantly commit

*when playing Chess. But here they do not feel the same re-
sponsibility. A game of Chess means to them a new and
happy freedom of mind. They may know the strict general
rules of Chess strategy, but they often indulge in all sorts of
hazardous combinations, consciously violating the rules, but
feeling happy in the carefree play of their imagination.*

*In this freedom, I think, lies the aesthetic quality of Chess.
A good game does not only satisfy our sense of logic, but also
our desire for beauty. Kant, in his* Critique of Judgement, *says
that beauty results from "a harmonious interplay of all the
different faculties of the human mind." When judgement
and understanding are interwoven with fancy and imagination, helping and completing each other, there arises that
perfect harmony of mind and sense perception, which is the
outstanding feature of our feeling of beauty. We may apply
this criterion of beauty very well to a game of Chess. Here
too, understanding and imagination are constantly cooperating and, in a certain sense, correcting each other. Thus the
pleasure we feel in playing Chess is perhaps a rather complicated phenomenon which arises from various sources, but
this multiplicity, no doubt, enhances our pleasure.*

*Chess has often been condemned as one-sided. I con-
sider this accusation quite unfounded and believe, on the
contrary, that it is just the many-sidedness of Chess which
gives it its high rank.*

*I am not certain, my dear Edward, whether you will agree
with me in this appreciation and justification of Chess, or
whether you will consider it a travesty on the real art of the
game. But I could only describe to you my own way of playing and enjoying Chess, though it may appear to you as a
very amateurish conception. As a matter of fact, when engaged in a game, I always have the secret feeling that I am
not playing Chess, but that I am playing with the thought
and the ideal of being a Chess master, an ideal which I can*

never attain but which, nevertheless, like other unfilled ideals and desires, gives me the greatest satisfaction.

I am awaiting the appearance of your new book with much interest; without doubt it will give me the same pleasure as your Chess Strategy *which I read about twenty-five years ago.*

With kind regards,

Yours,

ERNST CASSIRER

FROM A PHYSICIST:

John R. Bowman, Ph.D., is doing research work at the Mellon Institute in Pittsburgh. In building his Mass-Spectrograph he solved problems the difficulty of which can hardly be matched on the Chess board. He also wrote a book on beetles, entitled "The Pselaphidae of North America."

Dear Ed:

To me Chess is not a scientific game. That term should be confined to ones like Dominoes and Backgammon. Such games may be completely understood, because they are governed by definite laws which may be used for the determination of the best play in any given situation. Consequently, perfect play is attainable, individual skill is non-existent, and chance, in cumbersome disguise, is the controlling influence.

The perfect game of Chess has not yet been played, and never will be by a human mind. Basically, the game is as resolvable as tic-tack-toe, but the complete analysis is of such nearly infinite magnitude that formulation is impossible. It is this impossibility of knowing the best move that raises Chess from a scientific game to an art, a medium of individual ex-

pression. *Excluding athletic competitions, Chess is one of the very few games of skill in the true sense of the word.*

Not that the game is unscientific. It, like all the other arts, lies in an abstract matrix of law. Like in the other arts, we cannot comprehend all of these laws, but we can classify them and generalize. The understanding of these generalizations, the underlying principles of the game, is the stock-in-trade of the master player, without which strong play is impossible. But such an understanding is not sufficient; more is required than technique and knowledge of harmony to make a musician. The generalizations are neither complete nor infallible, and the player must exercise imaginative judgement, a fruit of experience, to make what seems to him the best move. This necessity for self-expression makes Chess a living art, and one of the finest intellectual games.

Yours sincerely,

John R. Bowman

JOHN R. BOWMAN

FROM A WOMAN:

This heading may seem somewhat comprehensive; but Leonore Gallet, who graduated from High School at the age of 12 and was awarded a scholarship by the famous teacher of Violinists, Leopold Auer, when 14, excels in more than one field and is thus well qualified to give the Woman's viewpoint.

Dear Edward,

Until I received your letter I had never considered why I liked Chess. I just enjoyed playing it; perhaps because in Chess at least, as distinguished from life, the Queen is given greater freedom and power than the King.

Speaking seriously, the appeal probably stems from the fact that Chess lets one enter a realm of phantasy in which one can carry out the things she dreams about without being hampered by the limitations imposed upon women in most fields of endeavor.

I don't consider it possible for any woman, though, to become a Chess master. She won't be able to keep her mind on the game long enough without letting her thoughts wander. When she thinks of a beautiful move she is liable to think also about how beautiful she looks in making it. Then there is that sale she saw advertised! Oh, and so many other things!

You always say Chess trains one to concentrate. I don't believe a word of it!

Yours sincerely,

Leonore Gallet

LEONORE GALLET

Contents

1.

CHESS FOR

FUN

Chess Amenities

HESS IS A LOT OF FUN
if you bring to it the right attitude and a sense of humor.
Of course, what is considered fun depends a good deal
on the intellectual level and the emotional make-up of
the person to be amused, just as in any other type of
recreation. I recall a nice comparison a friend of mine
once drew between the fun in Chess and the pleasure a
smoker derives from his cigarette. One man will smoke
one after another just for the kick he gets out of the taste.
Another—an artist perhaps—will blow rings and enjoy
the various shapes they assume and associate them with
forms he has used or might use some day in his work. A
scientist, watching the ashes on his cigarette grow longer
and longer, might muse on the transformations of energy
or the chemical changes taking place in that little roll of
tobacco.

Similarly, there are Chess players who play game after game just for the fight there is in them. To others, the beauty of a combination, the crystal clear logic of a maneuver carried through, appeals more than mere victory. A scientist might be intrigued by discovering in the game curious applications of physical laws which govern the conversion of potential into kinetic energy as the various Chessmen execute their threats. The military strategist might draw parallels between the applications of his maxims to real war and to the bloodless battle on the Chess board.

When it comes to getting fun out of Chess it does not really matter how well you play. If you do not like to be beaten with monotonous regularity you can always find someone who plays as badly as you do. And you can gloat over your victories and find excuses for your defeats in much the same manner as has been practised since dim antiquity by players much better than yourself—not excluding some of the masters of the game.

There are people who consider playing any game, including Chess, pure waste of time. I cannot help smiling when I hear someone voice that opinion. It makes me think of a fine remark with which Clarence Darrow introduced a talk on his favorite books. He said: "We are born and we die; and between these two most important events of our lives more or less time elapses which we have to waste somehow or other. In the end it does not seem to matter much whether we have done so in making money, or practising law, or reading, or playing, or in any other way, as long as we felt we were deriving a maximum of happiness out of our doings."

I quite agree with him. I do not blame anyone for

wasting his time the way he likes it best; although, of course, it is my private opinion that my own time-wasting plan, which includes a moderate dose of Chess, is the best.

If an Einstein thinks playing games too trivial I can appreciate it. The truly great ones of this world have good reason to be jealous of their every minute, for mankind's progress is bound up with their endeavor. But the disdain of games in the average mortal is apt to indicate merely a somewhat unbalanced opinion of the importance of things.

When I was very young I took Chess very seriously. Morning, noon and night I toiled to gain the knowledge which would equip me for the arduous road to mastership. My mother, to me quite inconceivably, did not share my view that there could be no higher task than to become a master of the Royal game. What my best friends said to me, in unmincing terms, when due to too much Chess it took me two years longer than it should have to graduate from the university, was not so flattering either.

However, I do not really regret that I spent much more time at Chess than I would counsel parents today to let their children take away from school work. For it was Chess which helped me out of the concentration camps of Europe during the first World War and took me to the United States; and it was Chess again through which I made most worth while contacts in my new country and in a score of years found many cherished friends. Too bad that some of them have gone where Chess no longer relieves monotony!

What pleasure it was, to see Michelson, the famous physicist, completely abandon himself at Chess which he played as badly as he played it passionately! What fun to argue with Arthur Brisbane about the value of Chess as training for the mind! I knew, although he never confessed it to me, that at one time he was so completely hypnotized by the game that he played it nights on end and was finally faced by the decision to give up either Chess or writing. He was fond of quoting the story of three newsboys who worked together in Detroit. One of them liked to play Chess; the other two preferred shooting dice. Twenty years later the boy who played Chess owned a newspaper while the other two had landed in jail. Brisbane would not concede that Chess had helped shaping the mental qualities of the newspaper owner. He said the boy had evidently had a good mind to start with or he would not have been attracted to Chess. I took the opposite stand, but I forget who won the argument.

While I said that the fun derived from playing Chess depends a good deal upon the mental make-up of the player, I am not blind to the fact that winning the game gives almost every one the greatest pleasure. The manner in which victory is achieved, whether by a beautiful combination or by brutal slaughter, seems to be only a secondary consideration. In the heat of battle the furtive —if unconscious—thought arises even in a scientist's mind, that the outcome might be teasingly used against him as a comparative measure of intelligence. After cooling down he would reject such thought with justified amusement.

After all, in a two-handed game there can be only one winner, and it is not necessarily always the better player who wins. He might be lured into a combination which turns out wrong though it would have been very beautiful had it worked out as intended. This should be sufficient solace; and the means other than skill—sometimes amusing and sometimes otherwise—which have been employed, and are still being employed here and there among Chess players to assure themselves of victory, seem highly dubious.

Damiano and Ruy Lopez, the top-ranking players of Italy and Spain in the sixteenth century, both recommended in their text books, without a trace of humor, that their students should always try to place the board so that the sun or the lamp would shine into their opponent's eyes! I regret that similar indelicate attempts at disconcerting the adversary have not altogether disappeared from Chess in our day. I remember receiving a challenge for a match from a player, accompanied by elaborate conditions, one of which was that he could smoke as much as he liked and keep the windows of the play room closed. Evidently he had heard that I was allergic to the substitution of nicotine for oxygen.

Fortunately less obvious methods have gradually gained favor, and though some players have quite a reputation for talking, whistling or singing their adversary out of a game, we are today inclined to consider it merely an unconscious outburst of cheerfulness on the part of our opponent, if he hums snatches of his favorite airs during a game and drums with his fingers on the table by way of accompaniment.

If you are fond of music you might even like that type of accompaniment to your play. But when playing in a club, where other games besides your own are in progress, it is necessary to consider among other things that musical tastes differ.

I hope I may be forgiven for taking this opportunity of recording a delightful conversation I once overheard, between two players who daily frequented the Manhattan Chess Club in New York. One of them, a young Canadian, used to whistle the theme of the Andante of Beethoven's violin concerto whenever he had a good position. Since he was one of the strongest players in the Club, most of its members had ample occasion to familiarize themselves with this Beethoven theme. The other player was a Supreme Court Judge with literary leanings, who, when he felt he had the better of the game, rarely omitted a chance to comment upon a move with a Shakespearean quotation. When attacking a piece he would say: "Get thee gone, Mortimer, get thee gone!" and when his own Queen was attacked he would ask: "Why appear you with this 'ridiculous boldness before Mylady?"

One day an ominous silence reigned at the Judge's table, while the Canadian, on the neighboring table, repeated the glorious Beethoven melody over and over with increasing enthusiasm. Finally the Judge growled: "Change the tune, Sir! It makes me lose my game!" The Canadian was startled into silence. Then he grew pensive and after fully a minute or two he turned and replied: "No, it's too good to be changed!"

Unfortunately, arguments among Chess players are not always so good-natured, and bad sportsmanship is no less common in Chess than in other contests. The degree to which it is sometimes carried in tournaments is indeed quite appalling. Some contestants think nothing of showing adjourned positions to stronger players and asking their advice. In fact, they have grown so accustomed to this unfair practice they are almost no longer capable of realizing that what they do is just plain cheating, whether sanctioned by usage or not.

I am glad to say, however, that the disease of bad sportsmanship is usually encountered in much less malignant form. It is true, you are almost sure to come up against the player who, no matter how often or how badly he loses, will always prove to you after the game is over that he could have won with ease; or against the player who after losing two or three games will discover a splitting headache which made it impossible for him to concentrate. Well, you need not be overly alarmed at the state of health of the latter, nor need you argue much with the former. Just beat him once more!

To bad losers I can give only this advice: Avoid Chess, for you will be beaten very frequently! If you must play the game and you feel the urge to explain away a loss, consider the temptation for your opponent to do the same thing should you win the next encounter. Or, console yourself with the reply a friend of mine once gave a member of his club who wailed how many won games he had thrown away that evening. He said: "Don't take it so hard! The Chess players are all complaining this year!"

Unsporting behavior among masters, I readily admit, is often due only to nervous tension on the part of the players and may be dismissed with a smile. I recall a most amusing incident of this kind which occurred in an offhand game between Nimzovich and Emanuel Lasker in Berlin. Nimzovich was very sensitive to smoke. Lasker, on the other hand, used to smoke one cigar after another while playing. However, he had consented good-naturedly not to smoke during this particular game. To Nim-

zovich's amazement he pulled out a big cigar after hardly
five or six moves had been made, bit off the end and put
it in his mouth. Nimzovich jumped up from his chair and
excitedly protested to the umpire: "Lasker made an ar-
rangement with me not to smoke and now look what he
is doing!" The umpire looked and said: "Well, he is not
smoking! The cigar is not lit!" "Ah!" retorted Nimzovich,
"But he *threatens* to smoke! And you know yourself that
Lasker has often said he considers a threat stronger than
its execution!"

It is hardly necessary to emphasize that while a good,
hard fight is what most players enjoy best, all fighting
should be strictly confined to the Chess board. Only if you
can ascribe your victory to your intelligent and coura-
geous play rather than to trickery, can you enjoy it without secret misgivings. It would be a mistake, of course, to
think that courage and intelligence are all that is needed
to make a good Chess player. A little work is also required,
as in any other endeavor which is really worth while.
This is what almost every beginner fails to consider. As
soon as he has learned how the Chessmen move, he wants
to play a game. He does not realize that such an attempt
is as hopeless as it would be for a music student to write
a symphony after he has barely acquainted himself with
the tone qualities of the different instruments. To become
a composer a musician must be thoroughly familiar with
the capabilities of each instrument and with the varied effects obtainable through their combination; and to be able
to play a real game of Chess the beginner must first learn
what each piece can accomplish by itself and in combination with others.

It is quite true that both can probably gain a great deal

of the necessary knowledge through trial and error and since, in fact, this groping in the dark is very pleasant I would not think of discouraging it.

Although almost all games of beginners present a chaotic mix-up of disconnected combinations, some method seems discernible in this madness. Common to all of them we note an early urge to storm forward with the Pawns. From their inferiority the beginner does not follow that it must be preferable to utilize the greater fighting power of his own pieces, but he tries to attack and catch his opponent's pieces with his Pawns in an attempt to diminish the fighting power of the adversary. In any case, he makes his combinations usually in the hope that the opponent will not see them, and in turn pays very little attention to the latter's moves. After he has lost most of his Pawns, he turns to his officers. He is always partial to the Queen and the Knight. To the Queen on account of her tremendous mobility, and to the Knight on account of his crooked jump which seems particularly suited to surprise the enemy. With one move he plans to win a piece, with the next to drive the hostile King into a mating net, no matter how many defensive forces bar the way, and so the game progresses, planless but exciting.

Gradually the beginner learns to anticipate certain constellations of pieces which have often proved fatal to him; he recognizes threats and begins to calculate more correctly. However, this empirical method naturally involves a considerable waste of time, which can be avoided by studying these dangerous combinations from a book presenting them in condensed form.

It might be argued that so many thousands of combinations are possible on the Chess board that it would be a hopeless task to catalogue them all. In reality, however, comparatively few of all possible combinations have a chance to occur in an actual game, and it is surprisingly simple to classify them in categories which can be readily remembered.

I have tried to illustrate these types in Chapters 3 and 4 in an informal manner which I felt would prove more amusing than a painstaking analysis but would in the end accomplish the same purpose.

After absorbing how the different pieces cooperate in these combinations, a player could conduct a whole game more or less intelligently; however, he would still find himself severely handicapped when meeting an opponent of equally limited experience but who understands the fundamental principles of Chess strategy. These principles govern all maneuvers on the Chess board and their grasp is essential if one is to recognize the most promising of the several plans which occur to a player on almost every move and which sometimes seem equally tempting to him.

It is really the comprehension of these principles which characterizes the difference between a strong and a weak player. An attempt to find out the laws of Chess strategy from personal experience in playing innumerable games is almost sure to result in failure. Acquainting oneself with them through a book which summarizes the distilled experience of generations of masters will naturally again save a tremendous amount of effort. I have devoted Chapter 5 to such a summary while illustrating the application of the strategic principles to actual games in Chapter 6.

Those who derive pleasure from subtle combinations,

even when there is no likelihood that they will ever occur in a game, will enjoy Chapter 7 in which the principal types of problems are discussed.

I have purposely not devoted a special chapter to list-
ing the different openings, an analysis of which forms
the essence of most older Chess books. Their proper
treatment is merely indicated during the discussion of
strategic principles. Their thorough study certainly does
not belong under the heading of fun, though it may help
some players to acquire mechanically the art of opening
their game in a style far above their real strength. However, once their recollection of "book-moves" is exhausted, they usually go to pieces if opposed by a player
of genuine talent for the game, who knows no analyzed
variations but who fights most nobly if he can stagger
through the opening without falling into a trap.

In the exposition of combinatory play as well as in the
discussion of the general principles governing positional
maneuvers I have tried to avoid all appeal to memory.
A mere perusal of these pages—preferably with another
player across the Chess board—will give a talented
student all he needs to progress rapidly by himself. To
those who do not care to devote to Chess the study it
takes to become a truly strong player, it will at least con-
vey an understanding of the motives behind the moves
of the masters, and it will thus contribute to their enjoyment of the game.

When playing with stronger players for the fun and
excitement of the battle rather than for the sake of in-
struction, reasonable odds will make the chances even
enough to give the weaker player the pleasure of oc-
casional victory. However, there is no sense in making

the odds so great that only an outright blunder can lose
the game. I should not recommend odds of more than
a Knight or at most a Rook. It is quite likely that here
and there you will win even with insufficient odds against
a much stronger player, because trusting in his superior
skill he will often try sacrificing combinations which are
unsound. When you have weathered the storm and find
yourself with an advantage in material which should be
decisive, do not attempt an early checkmate. Play with
the same care as if you had no advantage. Remember
your opponent sees everything you see and probably
much more. Consider any advanced Pawns of his as potential Queens and do away with them first, before pro-
ceeding against the King. The game may thus last longer,
but winning is a very pleasant pastime.

Chess Master, Artist & Scientist

AM OFTEN ASKED WHAT qualities make a good Chess player. In answering this question I would have to draw the same line of distinction which is indicated by the title of this book. No mysterious qualities such as great subtlety or a mathematical mind are required to play the "Chess for fun" type of the game tolerably well. As in any other mental activity, intelligence and imagination are the best assets.

What qualities a Chess player must have to become a master of the game is quite a different story. An excellent memory and great power of concentration are indispensable for him, and to some degree at least he must possess the creative ability we find in the real artist and scientist, who combines known elements into ever changing unexpected new forms.

Ernst Cassirer once said to me jokingly that what

Chess has in common with Science and Fine Art is its utter uselessness. I am sure I discerned a note of praise in this remark which was not unconscious. If one were to condemn Chess just because it is useless in the utilitarian sense of the word, one might, on the same basis, reject all but commercial art and many branches of higher mathematics which can hardly have any practical application.

I believe comparatively few people realize that, as paradoxical as it sounds, not only the artist but also the scientist, particularly the mathematician, often gets most pleasure out of working on very "impractical" problems. These may thrill him just because their solutions guide him into unexpected beautiful pathways, and whether or not they are useful would be the least of his concerns.

Somehow mankind has always acknowledged this search after truth and beauty as great and noble, no matter how useless it may be. If we look into the hall of immortal fame, whom do we find? Outside of a few arch-rascals such as Alexander, Caesar and Napoleon who won their fame through the grand manner in which they sacrificed thousands of lives in war, we find only scientists, artists and writers.

Far be it from me to claim this exalted place also for Chess masters. But the truly great ones among them are certainly endowed with the same mental faculties which distinguish great artists and great scientists, though public opinion usually thinks of a Chess master rather as an outstanding figure in the world of sports. The reason is that people in general misunderstand the mental processes of the Chess master as completely as they do those of the mathematician.

Wealthy industrialists may endow chairs of mathematics at our universities; but I am sure most of them do this only because they esteem the scientific qualities of the mathematician's mind which distinguish him from the rest of us and which should be valuable to industry; they probably would care little about the artistic qualities which his mind may have, but which the mathematician himself prizes much more. In fact, I have the suspicion that there would be little inclination to support the mathematician if it were generally known that he is usually much happier reveling in "mathematics for mathematics' sake" than pursuing the solutions of useful problems. The average person who has little or no artistic sensibility would hardly appreciate this type of work, just as he has little patience with "art for art's sake." He looks in art only for representation of life and nature and does not follow the artist who creates forms unrelated to them.

This attitude probably explains why the Chess master is not usually ranked with the great artist or the great mathematician. Chess certainly seems utterly unrelated to life, if we disregard its more or less superficial similarity to warfare. It appears to exist solely for its own sake, and to devote one's life to Chess—there are quite a number of people who do—seems the most unpardonable waste of vital force.

Still, we cannot help admitting that sometimes Chess masters display a mental ability which has all the attributes of genius. Emanuel Lasker was as unquestionably a genius as Gauss, Bach or Van Gogh. But it cannot have been a specific Chess faculty of his mind which made him one. Chess was created by man and not by nature, and so we cannot be born with an especial gift for Chess. The Chess mind must naturally be related to other types which we are used to recognize in men outstanding in some of our more essential activities.

The Chess master must have a mind capable of scientific reasoning, just as the mathematician. Scientific reasoning rests not merely on logical thought. It also requires that mysterious faculty which we call intuition; without it no inductive thinking is possible of the kind that alone produces science, because in no other way can general laws be conceived which govern an infinity of special cases.

The same process of inductive thinking is required of the Chess master. Only if he is able to recognize general laws to which all his combinations are subordinate, can he rise above the class of the majority of Chess players who rely solely upon their experience and imagination.

Imagination, to be sure, is one of the most important requisites of a Chess master. He must be able to visualize positions in his mind before they actually occur, and he must be able to conceive combinations he has never seen before. Here we have the link between Chess master and artist.

Among the arts it is music with which Chess shows a most obvious relation. Like mathematics, music has hardly any connection with reality. It does not copy nature and does not necessarily require the experience of life. That is why once in a while Chess prodigies are born, and mathematical prodigies, and musical prodigies, but never children who can paint or write in a masterly fashion until they have matured.

Here we have another striking relation between Chess, mathematics and music which probably explains why Chess is the favorite pastime of many mathematicians and musicians, and of many among the very large number of people who like music or mathematics.

An interesting difference between them is that while mathematicians sometimes make very excellent Chess players musicians hardly ever do. Also, mathematicians usually like music but musicians do not like mathematics. What fascinates the musician in Chess is obviously the opportunity to exercise his imagination freely. In the parallels with scientific induction he is hardly ever interested.

I used to play a good deal of Chess with one of the famous violinists. After losing a game he would never listen to suggestions how to improve his strength by checking every idea, no matter how brilliant it seemed to him, from the point of view of the general strategic principles. He always wanted to play a new game immediately, to try out new ideas and revel in the realm of fantasy.

And so, every time we played, we went through veritable Chess orgies which thrilled him tremendously but in which he never consciously improved his game. And whenever he did win a game he was highly elated by the thought that he had invented a new combination; and I never had the heart to tell him that he had not won because he had played so well but because I had played so badly.

Checkmating Combinations

N EVERY GAME OF
Chess the players constantly keep two possible courses
before their minds: "Blitzkrieg" attacks aimed at checkmating the King in the middle of the game, and maneuvers designed to gain an advantage in material which
will tell in the ending.

Checkmating attacks, while usually involving a wilder
type of combination, are simpler to understand because
nothing need be considered but the naked task in hand,
that of felling the opposing King. It does not matter
whether in the course of executing this task material is
lost. In fact, more often than not material is sacrificed in
order to denude the King of defensive forces.

In all other types of combinations the situation on
every part of the board must be kept in mind constantly,
to make sure that the advantage sought with the ma-

neuver under consideration may not be offset by a greater disadvantage in another sector of the battle field.

Let us then first examine the characteristic roles which the different pieces play in checkmating combinations. When such combinations take place in the middle-game, the King to be checkmated is usually located in the corner or on the Kt sq of the side of the board on which he has castled, while the King of the winning player is not actively engaged. A Knight or a Bishop alone, or even in combination, have rarely occasion to give a checkmate. The following three examples illustrate practically all cases of this type which are ever encountered in practice.

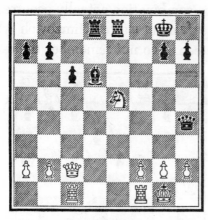

DIAGRAM 1.

In the position of Diagram 1 White would play 1. Q—Kt3 ch. Black can only reply K—R, for after K—B he would be mated through 2. Q—B7. Now White continues with 2. Kt—B7 ch, forcing the King back to Kt sq, where he is exposed to a discovered check. In giving such check the Knight could capture either the Rook or the Bishop. But White can checkmate in three moves starting with the double check 3. Kt—R6. After K—R a

neat Queen sacrifice follows: 4. Q—Kt8 ch. Black is
forced to capture the Queen with the Rook and in that
way to deprive his King of the only flight square.
5. Kt—B7 then checkmates him.

As far as I know the American Master Paul Morphy is
credited with the discovery of this "strangled mate" in
one of his games which at the time made a sensation. Today there are few players who are not familiar with it.

In conjunction with a Bishop who controls the squares
Kt7 and R8 the Knight has sometimes an opportunity
to checkmate on R6. Diagram 2 shows a position in
which such a mate is reached after a series of brilliant
sacrifices. This combination actually occurred in a game
played by the famous master Nimzovich when he was
a boy of eighteen. I do not remember the exact position

DIAGRAM 2.

of the men on the Queen's wing, but the pieces involved
in the combination were placed as in the diagram.

The idea which came to Nimzovich's mind was to
play Q—R6 in order to follow up P×Q with Kt—Kt4,
threatening mate on R6. However, Black could then save

himself with KR—K, securing a flight square for his King. To avoid this Nimzovitch hatched a beautiful plan. He played 1. B—K8 !! This threatens 2. B×P ch, R×B; 3. Q×R ch and mate on Kt7, and Black therefore accepted the sacrifice with QR×B. But now the King's Rook is hemmed in and after 2. Q—R6, P×Q; 3. Kt—Kt4 the checkmate on R6 cannot be guarded against.

Incidentally, it would not have helped Black to answer White's first move with P×B, because White would then have forced a mate with 2. P×P, threatening 3. Q—Kt5 ch and 4. Q—Kt7. 2. . . . ., K—R does not save him, since 3. Q—R6, R—KKt; 4. Kt×P again mates.

Our third example shows a mate with the Bishop, supported by a Knight, which may occur very early in the opening, and the unsuspecting beginner is not infre-

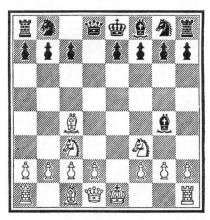

DIAGRAM 3.

quently trapped by a combination involving this mate. The position of Diagram 3 might be reached after the moves 1. P—K4, P—Q4; 2. P×P, Q×P; 3. QKt—B3, Q—Q; 4. Kt—B3, B—Kt5; 5. B—B4. White now threatens B×P ch, for after K×B he would regain the piece

with Kt—K5 ch and he would be a Pawn to the good.
Black can protect himself with 5. . . . ., P—K3. In a game
which I once played against a rather inexperienced opponent the position of the Diagram was reached and he
continued improperly with 5. . . . ., KKt—B3. This does
not defend the threat because after 6. B×P ch, K×B;
7. Kt—K5 ch White still regains his piece since Black's
Bishop is attacked twice and defended only once. In the
game in question I actually played 6. Kt—K5, my opponent captured my Queen, and I checkmated him with
7. B×P.

Had he looked before jumping at my Queen, he would
have played 6. . . . ., B—K3. He could not have played
B—R4 because I would have simply captured the Bishop
with 7. Q×B as after Kt×Q my Bishop would have again
mated on B7.

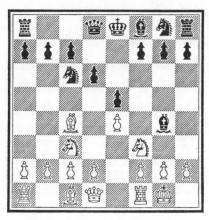

DIAGRAM 4.

Diagram 4 shows a position which belongs in the same
category, though the checkmating combination is a little
more complicated, involving (as it does) a Bishop and
two Knights. This position is reached very frequently in

actual games and therefore deserves especial mention. It is Black's move, and the advance Kt—Q5 seems tempting which attacks White's pinned Knight. However, White can again offer the sacrifice of his Queen: After Kt×P Black cannot capture the Queen as B×P ch, K—K2; and Kt—Q5 mate would follow.

In the great majority of cases mating attacks in the middle-game with Bishops and Knights are carried out with the cooperation of the Queen. This is quite natural, of course, since the Queen is the most powerful piece. The targets are almost always the King's Rook's Pawn and the King's Knight's Pawn as in the majority of games the King castles on the King's side of the board. The Rook's Pawn is more frequently the object of the onslaught because he can be readily attacked by the opposing King's Knight from his natural developing square KB3. In games in which White's first move P—K4 is answered with P—K3 (French defense) Black's Rook's Pawn is usually, in addition, attacked by White's King's Bishop, which is well placed on Q3, with his line of influence readily opened by the advance of the King's Pawn to K5.

Diagram 5 shows a position reached in the French defense rather frequently. It is Black's move. Castling at this stage would invite a most dangerous attack because the Rook's Pawn would then be defended only by the King while White's Bishop is already aiming at it and White's Knight and Queen can be brought up rapidly, too, against this very weak spot. As a matter of fact White would be able to force a win immediately. He would begin with 2. B×P ch, sacrificing his Bishop in order to open the Rook's file for his Queen. If, instead,

he started with Kt—KKt5 Black might possibly be able
to defend himself satisfactorily with P—KR3. Black has
the choice between accepting or rejecting the Bishop
sacrifice. Of course, if he rejects it and plays K—R,
White could simply withdraw the Bishop again and remain a Pawn ahead. He will therefore carefully examine
whether he can stand White's onslaught after K×B. The

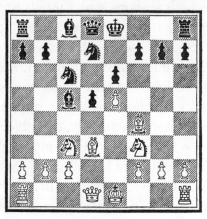

DIAGRAM 5.

consequence would be 3. Kt—Kt5 ch. Again Black has a
choice of moves. He could go back to Kt or come out to
Kt3. He cannot go to R sq because Q—R5 ch and mate
on R7 would follow. Neither can he go to R3 because
Kt×P would win the Queen through the discovered
check. If he retreats to Kt sq White checkmates in six
moves beginning with 4. Q—R5. To protect the mate on
R2 Black must reply R—K, whereupon White proceeds
with 5. Q×P ch, K—R; 6. Q—R5 ch, K—Kt; 7. Q—R7
ch, K—B; 8. Q—R8 ch, K—K2; and 9. Q×P mate.

It follows that after 3. Kt—Kt5 ch Black must play
K—Kt3. But now 4. Q—Q3 ch, P—B4; 5. Q—Kt3 or
Kt×KP or P×P e.p. would give White an overwhelming

attack which is bound to yield a winning advantage in material even though Black may avoid a forced mate.

The combination of the moves Kt—KKt5 and Q—KR5 is met with time and again and represents the typical use of the King's Knight for a mating attack. The Queen's Knight usually finds employment in such attacks either on Q5 or on KB5, after reaching the latter

DIAGRAM 6.

square from QB3 via K2 and KKt3 or from Q2 via KB and K3 or KKt3. On Q5 the Knight is placed particularly well if the opposing King's Knight is pinned on KB3 as in the position of Diagram 6. White's threat is to make a breach in the chain of Pawns which protect the King by exchanging on KB6 and then to plant his Queen on KR6. If Black, on the move, plays 1. ...., Kt—Q5, thus imitating White's maneuver, White would not exchange immediately, because after 2. B×Kt, P×B; 3. Q—Q2 Black could guard his KR3 by K—Kt2 and thereby prevent the cooperation of White's Queen and Knight. Instead, White would play 2. Q—Q2 first. This move cannot be refuted by B×Kt, for White does not recapture but carries out his original threat: 3. B×Kt. Now P×B would be followed by Q—R6 and Kt×KBP, winning Black's Queen who must sacrifice herself to stave off the mate on R2.

On the other hand, Black would lose his Queen also after 3. ...., Q—Q2. White would continue with 4. Kt—K7 ch and if Black does not give up the Queen for the Knight but moves the King White checkmates neatly with 5. B×P ch, K×B; 6. Q—Kt5 ch, K—R; 7. Q—B6.

From these considerations it is evident that after White's initial 2. Q—Q2 Black must play something different from B×Kt. He might try P—B3 in order to dislodge White's disagreeable Knight. But after 3. Kt×Kt ch, P×Kt White plays 4. B—R4! and again threatens to occupy the square KR6 with his Queen. The position reached is shown in Diagram 7.

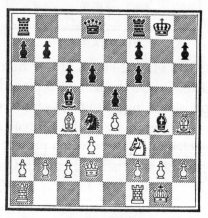

DIAGRAM 7.

Black's best defense is probably again 4. ...., K—Kt2, to prevent White's Queen from cooperating with the Bishop in the attack on Black's pinned Pawn. To try to win a Pawn instead by playing 4. ...., B×Kt; 5.

Q—R6, Kt—K7 ch; 6. K—R, B×P ch; 7. K×B, Kt—B5 ch; 8. K—R, Kt—Kt3 would be a very dangerous thing to do, because it would enable White's Rooks to enter the battle. We will not discuss this question here because

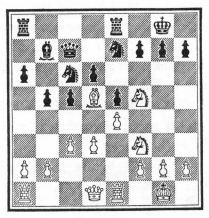

DIAGRAM 8.

it involves the understanding of general principles which we have not as yet stated. Chapter 5 will furnish the explanation.

Diagram 8 illustrates a case in which both the King's and Queen's Knight take part in the assault on the opposing King. The most obvious move for White would be 1. Kt—Kt5, attacking B7 and preparing for the old favorite Q—R5. This line of play would indeed be very strong, for after Kt×B; 2. P×Kt Black must move his Knight and it is not very likely that after 3. Q—R5 he will be able to stand the combined attack of the white forces lined up against him. If he played 2. ...., Kt—Q, for example, 3. Q—R5, P—KR3; and 4. R—K3 would spell his early doom. He could not capture the Knight because 5. R—R3 would lead to a mate. If he played B×P, 5. R—Kt3 would follow, threatening 6. Kt×P ch etc.

Black's best chance would be 2. ...., Kt—K2; 3. Q—
R5, Kt×Kt; 4. Q×RP ch, K—B; 5. Q×Kt, B×P. But
6. Kt—R7 ch, K—Kt; 7. Q—R5 followed by R—K3
would prove very annoying.

Master Teichmann, who had the position of the Diagram against Schlechter in the great Karlsbad tournament of 1911, played more decisively 1. B×P ch ! K×B;
2. Kt—Kt5 ch, Black must now go back to Kt sq because
if he came out to B3 White would play 3. Kt×P ch,
K—B2; 4. Kt—Kt5 ch, K—B3; 5. Kt×KtP ! and neither
one of the Knights could be captured by Black as Kt—
K6 ch would win the Queen.

After 2. ...., K—Kt White continued 3. Q—R5,
Kt×Kt; 4. Q×P ch, K—B; 5. Q×Kt ch, K—Kt; 6. Q—
Kt6 !! and Black resigned as there is nothing to be done
against the threat R—K3—R3—R8 ch and Q—R7 mate.
Indeed a subtle finish. Had White played 6. R—K3 then
Black might have been able to hold out by sacrificing
his KtP with P—Kt3 and then interposing his Queen on
Kt2.

Mating attacks in which a Rook makes the final assault after a line has been opened for him through the
sacrifice of a piece for the Knight's Pawn or Rook's Pawn
represent perhaps the most frequent type. Diagram 9
shows a position in which two pieces are sacrificed in
order to open both the Rook's and the Knight's file. This
position occurred in a game between Emanuel Lasker
and Bauer at Amsterdam in 1889 and has served as a
brilliant example for combinations in similar cases. The
advantage of White's position lies in the ability of the
King's Rook to enter the fray via KB3. Lasker started
with 1. Kt—R5, threatening to take twice on KB6 and

in that way to open the King's Knight file. After Kt×Kt he did not recapture but immediately tore the Black King's position open: 2. B×P ch, K×B; 3. Q×Kt ch, K—Kt; 4. B×P !! The point of the combination. Black is forced to take, because P—B4 is answered by 5. B—K5 ! with the threat 6. Q—Kt6 ch. Neither 5. . . . ., Q—K

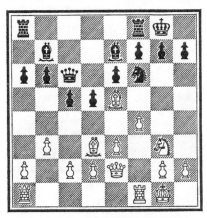

DIAGRAM 9.

would then help, on account of Q—R8 ch and mate on R7, nor 5. . . . ., R—B3, on account of R—B3 and R—Kt3 ch.

After 4. . . . ., K×B the game proceeded as follows: 5. Q—Kt4 ch, K—R2; 6. R—B3, P—K4; 7. R—R3 ch, Q—R3; 8. R×Q ch, K×R; 9. Q—Q7 and White won another piece.

By a strange coincidence almost exactly the same combination occurred twenty five years later in a game Nimzovich—Tarrasch at St. Petersburg. Diagram 10 shows the crucial position in that game. Tarrasch played P—Q5, and after 2. P×P he continued, like Emanuel Lasker in the position of Diagram 9, B×P ch; 3. K×B, Q—R5 ch; 4. K—Kt, B×P ! This time the King cannot

capture the Bishop at all, as Q—Kt5 ch and R—Q4
would force a mate in few moves. The game proceeded
as follows: 5. P—B3, KR—K ! Now K×B would be answered by R—K7 ch and mate in two moves. 6. Kt—K4,

DIAGRAM 10.

Q—R8 ch; 7. K—B2, B×R. White cannot recapture because Q—R7 ch would win the Queen. Thus, Black has
already obtained a superiority in material. However,
after White's next move the position is still full of tricky
threats and if Black tried to win the ending after sim-
plifying the game by exchanging Queens with Q—Kt7
ch etc., he would find it by no means easy. Instead, he
plays for a mate and the manner in which he proceeds
is very instructive. It is typical for cases in which the
King is driven out into the open and deserves careful
study. Diagram 11 shows the position reached after
Black's seventh move.

White played 8. P—Q5, which opens the long diagonal for his Bishop and threatens Q—B3 and Q—Kt7
mate. The reason why Black did not counter this threat
with Q—Kt7 ch and Q×Q is that after the exchange his

Bishop is attacked and if he withdraws then White's King returns to B2 whereupon Black cannot prevent the loss of the exchange through Kt—B6. On the other hand, if Black, after exchanging Queens, plays P—B4 and

DIAGRAM 11.

takes the Knight in return for his Bishop, White continues with R×P and his advanced Queen's Pawn becomes quite threatening.

Black's actual continuation is much stronger: 8. . . . . , P—B4; 9. Q—B3, Q—Kt7 ch; 10. K—K3, R×Kt ch ! 11. P×R, P—B5 ch. This leads to a forced mate in five moves. In the heat of the battle Black overlooks a mate in three through Q—Kt6 etc. 12. K×P, R—B ch; 13. K—K5, Q—R7 ch; 14. K—K6, R—K ch; 15. K—Q7, B—Kt4 mate.

The reader will have noticed that in practically all of the mating attacks discussed the Queen and the majority of the other pieces of the defending King were placed too far away to help in time. Positions of this type fairly invite sacrificial combinations, though experience has shown that as long as the King's Knight is on KB3 from

where he protects the weak square KR2, and as long as
a Rook is handy for defense, it is often extremely difficult to overwhelm the King even with a greatly superior
force. A massive Pawn wall in front of the King is not
necessarily an adequate defense against an accumula-
tion of hostile pieces. In the position of Diagram 12,
taken from a game Rogosin—Edward Lasker played at
New York 1940, we see such a Pawn wall successfully
demolished in spite of the presence of the protecting
King's Knight.

A glance at the position shows much greater mobility of the Black forces. The placement of Black's
Queen and White's King in the same diagonal suggests
the idea to sacrifice the Bishop on Kt6 so that the Queen

DIAGRAM 12.

can take the King's Pawn with check after White has
captured the Bishop. Then Black's Knight can cooperate
from Kt5.

But what if after **1. ...., B×P; 2. P×B, Q×P ch; 3.
K—R, Kt—Kt5** White defends the check threatened on
his KB2 by **4. R—Q2?** In answer to Q—R3 ch White

would move to Kt sq and R—K6 followed by R×Kt would be no real threat because in recapturing with his Knight's Pawn White would be defending his KR2 with his Rook. I was just about ready to abandon the idea of the Bishop sacrifice when it occurred to me that I could lure the protecting King's Knight away with the Rook sacrifice 4. . . . ., R—K4 !! Lure is not really the word, for White must accept the proffered gift. The threat is 5. . . . ., R—R4 ch, 6. Kt—R4, R×Kt ch; 7. P×R, Q—Kt6; 8. K—Kt, Q—R7 ch; 9. K—B, Q—R8 ch; 10. K—K2, Q×KtP ch; 11. K—K (Not K—Q because of Kt—K6 ch followed by Q—Kt8 ch and mate through either B—Kt5 or Q×R) Q—Kt8 ch; 12. B—B, R—K ch; 13. R—K2, R×R ch; 14. K×R, Q—K6 ch; 15. K—Q, Kt—B7 ch; 16. K—B2, B—B4 ch; 17. B—Q3 and Q×B mate.

Evidently my opponent saw this forced mate too, for he played 5. Kt×R. While I can now attack his King with my Queen and Knight in the same manner as just indicated, his Knight blocks the King's file and protects the square Kt4. The position reached at this stage is given in Diagram 13.

White is a Rook and a Knight ahead, but he has a Rook, a Knight and the Queen practically out of play, so that Black in reality attacks with a greater force than White can muster for defense. The game continued: 5. . . . ., Q—R3 ch; 6. K—Kt, Q—R7 ch; 7. K—B, Q—R8 ch; 8. K—K2, Q×P ch; 9. K—Q, Kt—K6 ch; 10. K—K, Q×P ch; 11. K—K2, Q×Kt; 12. K—B2.

The great temptation was now to play Q—R7 ch, sacrificing the Knight also. After 13. K×Kt, Q—Kt6 ch; 14. K—Q4, Q—B5 ch, however, I could not see a deci-

sive continuation in case White should give up the
Bishop with 15. B—K4. Neither could I see a forced
mate after 13. ...., R—K ch, 14. K—B3.

I therefore chose the safer Q—B5 ch; 13. K—Kt,

DIAGRAM 13.

Q—Kt6 ch; 14. K—R, B—Kt5. It is true, White is still
a Rook down, but it is most unlikely that the denuded
King will escape alive. White defended the threatened
Bishop check with 15. Kt—Q4 and I attacked the defending Knight with Q—B5. White can protect the
Knight only by moving the Bishop, but the latter has
not many moves to choose from. B—K2 would lose a
piece because after B×B White would have to recapture with the Rook, leaving the Knight unprotected; for
if Kt×B, Q—B6 followed by Q—Kt7 mates. Neither
can the Bishop go to B sq, on account of Kt×B with attack on the Rook by the Queen. Nor does B—B2 look
good, since R—QB would follow. For these reasons
White decided on 16. B—Kt5, which keeps the black
Rook from K sq. From there he could attack the white
King via K4—R4.

With K sq inaccessible the Bishop file remains the only one through which the Rook can make his way to the battle field, and in that file the square B5 is the only desirable one. I therefore played first P—QR3, and after 17. B—R4 I followed up with R—QB. White then played 18. Q—Q3, and it looked as if he would succeed at last in getting his Queen's Rook to work. However, after R—B5 White must first defend the threat R×Kt and B—B6 ch etc., and at the same time he must protect his Bishop. The only move to do this is 19. B—Q, but this shuts out the Queen's Rook again and Black has time for the devastating move Kt—B4. The entry of Black's Rook into the hand to hand fight can no longer be blocked. 20. Kt×Kt, B×Kt; 21. Q—K2, Q—Kt6, and the threat R—R5 cannot be defended. The game actually went on to the mate: 22. Q—K8 ch, K—Kt2; 23. R—Kt2, B—K5; 24. B—B3 (if Q×B, Q—R6 ch wins), B×B; 25. QR—KKt. The Queen's Rook makes a move after all. But it is too late: 25. ...., Q—R6 mate.

The foregoing examples will have given the reader a fair idea as to how the different pieces cooperate in mating attacks; and as all positions were taken from actual games they will also have served to show to some extent what squares are the most suitable for these pieces in opening and early middle-game to be well placed for future attacking operations.

However, as pointed out in the beginning of this chapter, most games do not lead to a mate at an early stage but are won in the ending, i.e. after the majority of the pieces have disappeared from the board and only one or two are left in addition to King and Pawns. In order to be able to decide, therefore, what course to steer in middle-games which due to a fairly balanced position preclude violent action, we must necessarily know something about the characteristics of favorable and unfavorable end-games. Typical examples of the most important endings are discussed in the following chapter. None of them need be committed to memory except that of King and Pawn against King. The others are intended more as an aid in forming a clearer idea of the value of the different pieces, which really cannot be fully appreciated until the final phase of the game has been reached. Here their true character is unmasked and their strength as well as their weakness shows itself unmistakably on the open board from which the bodies of their dead comrades have been removed.

End-Game Play

OST CHESS
players pay too little attention to endings. They consider
them a dull part of the game because there are not enough
pieces left to make the wild sacrificing combinations
likely which attract them most to Chess. Besides, they
think they can easily master end-game positions with
their relatively few pieces after they have learned how
to make combinations with many men.

Well, they are mistaken. The end-game harbors some
of the most surprising maneuvers on the Chess board,
quite different in type from those in opening and mid-
game, because King and Pawns play the leading role
while in the earlier stages their activity is subordinate
to that of the pieces.

The study of end-games furthermore produces a much
better insight into the characteristic powers of each dif-

ferent piece. These characteristics are naturally more clearly accentuated in positions in which a piece is on its own, so to speak, rather than being aided by others.

The piece which survives the slaughter of the middle-game most frequently is the Rook, and Rook endings are therefore the most important to be acquainted with. Sometimes it is desirable to exchange them in order to reduce the position to a Pawn ending, and sometimes only avoiding their exchange will save a game. The decision of such problems, in turn, requires the understanding of pure Pawn endings, and it is with these, therefore, that I will start.

Strange as it seems, most amateurs do not even know when an ending with King and one Pawn against

DIAGRAM 14.

the King is won. But since the vast majority of all Chess games in which one of the players wins a Pawn could in all likelihood be reduced to just that type of ending, its clear understanding is indispensable. The only thing to remember, in order not to have to figure out this ending every time it may be reached, is that in the position

shown on the left of Diagram 14, where King and Pawn
are side by side on the sixth rank and the lone King occupies the queening square of the Pawn, the game is
drawn if it is the defending King's move, while it is won
if it is the Pawn's turn to advance.

After 1. P—Kt7 the King must go to R2, allowing
White's King to advance to B7 from where he guards
the queening square. But if it had been Black's turn to
play a stalemate would be reached after K—B; 2. P—Kt7
ch, K—Kt; 3. K—Kt6.

It follows that in the position shown on the right side
of the Diagram White, on the move, must not advance
his Pawn. He can win only by playing 1. K—B6, K—Kt;
2. K—K7, followed by the advance of the Pawn.

These cases could be summarized in the simplest manner by saying that with King and Pawn on the sixth rank
and the lone King on his first rank the player of the
Pawn can win only if he can advance the Pawn without
thereby checking the King. The only exception is the
Rook's Pawn, who cannot win even when advancing
without check, because a stalemate results.

Kings placed as in Diagram 15 are said to be "in opposition." They occupy the same file on squares of the same
color. In most cases it is desirable for either player to
reach opposition, and to be able to maintain it, with the
opponent's turn to play. If in the position on the left side
of the Diagram White advanced his Pawn two squares,
Black would reply K—B3 and White could not maintain
the opposition. The game would end in a draw, Black
defending himself as follows: 2. P—B5, K—B2; 3.
K—Kt5, K—Kt2; 4. P—B6 ch, K—B2; 5. K—B5, K—B;
6. K—Kt6, and the drawn position illustrated in Dia-

gram 14 has been reached. If Black had played K—Kt
on his 5th move he would lose, because after 6. K—Kt6,
K—B White advances the Pawn without check.

On his first move White should advance his Pawn
only one square. In answer to Black's K—B3 he can then
go into opposition with 2. K—B4 and force the gradual
advance of King and Pawn as in the right hand illustration of Diagram 14.

DIAGRAM 15.

The position on the right side of Diagram 15 requires
similar considerations. In order to win White must try
to reach opposition in front of his Pawn. 1. K—Kt4,
K—Kt3; Black has now obtained the opposition but
White drives him out of it again by 2. P—Kt3.

White could not accomplish the same purpose by first
advancing his Pawn one square. For after 1. P—Kt3
Black would play K—Kt2 ! If now White's King advances, Black goes into opposition. And if White tries
to maintain it by 2. K—B4, K—B3; 3. P—Kt4, Black
answers K—Kt3, and White's Pawn prevents the King
from opposing on Kt3. The game is therefore drawn.

The understanding of the tactical maneuvers which

may bring victory to the player who has gained the opposition of the Kings in pure Pawn endings is indispensable for the proper conduct of these endings. Nor does
one know, without it, when to allow a middle game to be
turned into a Pawn ending by the exchange of all pieces
and when to try to avoid such an exchange. The following examples show several typical situations of this kind.

In Diagram 16 Black can hold the game if he has the
opposition, i.e. if it is White's turn to move. White wins
easily if it is Black who must move and thus give up the
opposition. In reply to 1. . . . ., K—K4 the Bishop's Pawn
advances and the Knight's Pawn queens perforce. Nor
could Black stop White from capturing the Knight's

DIAGRAM 16.

Pawn if he retreated to the third rank: 1. . . . ., K—B3; 2.
K—K4 ! (Not 2. P—B4, P×P ch; 3. K×P, for K—Kt3 would
reduce the position to the case which the discussion of
Diagram 15 showed to end in a draw. Only if Black's
Rook's Pawn were still back at R3 could White now win
by running over to the King wing. He would catch
Black's Pawn in five moves. The black King, after cap-
turing White's passed Pawn, would get as far as K2 on

his fifth move, but then White would play K—Kt7 and his Rook's Pawn would queen. With the black Pawn on R4, however, White's King gets only as far as Kt6 on his sixth move, so that Black can answer K—B1 and reach the corner, blocking White's Pawn, unless White plays K—R7. Then Black draws the game by repeating the moves K—B1 and K—B2 which keep the white King in the Rook's file blocking his Pawn himself.)

After 2. K—K4, K—Q3 White has again the opposition and Black can't keep him from reaching B5 and winning the Pawn: 3. K—Q4, K—B3; 4. K—K5, K—B2; 5. K—Q5, K—Kt3; 6. K—Q6, K—Kt2; 7. K—B5, K—R3; 8. K—R6, and Black must abandon his Pawn. White then wins easily.

White on the move in the diagram can't avoid the draw. He could temporarily wrest opposition from Black with 1. P—B4 !, P×P ch; 2. K—B3, K—B3; 3. K×P, but Black regains it after K—Kt3 and stops the Knight's Pawn from queening, as the play in Diagram 15 demonstrated. Nor can White queen his Rook's Pawn. As shown above, Black gets over to the King's wing in time to prevent it.

Black must be careful not to let White trick him out of opposition by first retreating to the second rank in order to lure his King to B5. In reply to 1. K—B2, for example, Black must play K—B3 !, going into distant opposition, and not K—B5, when 2. K—Q2, K—Q4, would let White gain the opposition with 3. K—Q3.

Diagram 17 shows a position which I had in the first Chess tournament I ever played, at the age of eighteen. I shall never forget it because had I made the right move I would have won the Berlin championship. I had prematurely resigned myself to losing this game because my King is held on the Queen's wing by my opponent's passed Pawn, so that he can leisurely attack my Pawns with his King and queen one of his Pawns on the King's wing.

In that frame of mind I played half mechanically 1. P—B4 and resigned the game when Black replied P—B3, as the three black Pawns hold my four Pawns. If I advance my Knight's Pawn Black simply walks over to the King's wing.

DIAGRAM 17.

Had I carefully analyzed the consequences of 1. P—B6 !!, I would have probably seen that this move wins the game. After P×P; 2. P—B4 the threat is P—Kt5, freeing the Rook's Pawn, so that Black must play 2. ...., K—Q5; 3. P—Kt5, BP×P; 4. P×P, K—K4; 5. P×P, K—B3. But now comes the surprise: 6. K—B2 forces Black's King to move, and his own Pawn prevents him from reaching my Pawns. No matter where he moves, 7. P—R7 wins.

The memory of this endgame haunted me nineteen years later in one of the games of my match for the U. S. championship against Frank Marshall. The position of Diagram 18 had been reached, and of course I thought of P—B6 right away, followed by the advance of the other King's side Pawns. In this connection it occurred to me that I could give back the exchange which I had won early in the game, and get the black King out of play in that way, over on the Queen's Rook's file, so that my own King should have a free hand in the centre as

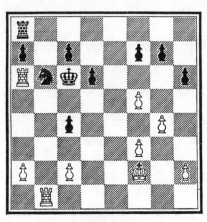

well as among the weakened Pawns of Black's King's wing. For these reasons I proceeded as follows: 1. P—B6, P×P; 2. P—QR4, P—Q4; 3. P—R5, K—Kt2; 4. P×Kt, K×R; 5. P×BP, R—QB; 6. K—K3, R×P; 7. K—Q4. So far so good. Black cannot attempt holding the Queen's Pawn, as R—Q2 would be answered by K—B5 with the threat K—B6. On the other hand there is no way for the Black King to get back into play unless he opposes the Rook on Kt2. After the exchange I will win the two black Pawns in the centre. If Black's King's side Pawns were not torn up and I had the threat of getting my Rook's Pawn free, the ending would be definitely won for Black, for he has the "distant passed Pawn." My King would finally land on the Queen's Rook's file and the Black King on the Queen's Bishop's file, two moves closer to the Pawns on the other wing. Probably Marshall hoped that an ending of this general type would develop.

The game continued as follows: 7. ...., R—Kt2; 8. R×R, K×R; 9. K×P, P—B6; Black probably thought of P—B4 here. But while P×P would then have eliminated my threat to free my Rook's Pawn, it would have created a new menace. My King would threaten to take the Bishop's Pawn via K5—B6. Black could not immediately advance the Queen's Rook's Pawn on account of K—B5 ! His best play would probably have been K—Kt3, leading to a very difficult ending. After Black's actual move my Rook's Pawn becomes so serious a threat that Black must rush to aid with his King, and the commanding position of my own King in the centre greatly reduces the value of Black's Queen's Rook's Pawn. The game continued: 10. P—R4, K—B2; 11. P—R5, K—Q2; 12. K—Q4, K—K3; 13. K×P. In this position, which is shown in Diagram 19, I simply threaten K—Kt4 followed by the advance of the Queen's Bishop's Pawn. The black King can no longer operate on the Queen's wing on account of my threat P—KB4 and P—KKt5, as in the position of Diagram 17. Black therefore takes his last chance to eliminate the menace involved in the advance of my Knight's Pawn, by playing 13. ...., P—B4. But just now I should have advanced the Knight's Pawn all the same. This sacrifice would have crowned the whole combination originally planned when I advanced the King's Bishop's Pawn to the sixth. However I suffered from the following hallucination: I saw that after 14. P—Kt5, P×P; 15. P—R6, K—B3; 16. K—Q4,

P—Kt5; 17. P—B4, P—Kt6; 18. K—K3, P—R4 my Bishop's Pawn would queen one move ahead of Black's Rook's Pawn, and that I would then win Black's Queen by Q—KR8 ch. I was just about to make my move, when I suddenly saw a variation of which I had not thought previously. Black could first queen his Knight's Pawn,

DIAGRAM 19.

thus forcing my King to Kt square, and then his Rook's Pawn would queen with a check, so that I had no more winning chance. I completely overlooked that I could do the very same thing, first forcing Black's King to KR sq by queening my Rook's Pawn. Then my Bishop's Pawn would queen with a check and Black would get no Queen at all!

The move I actually made also leads to a winning position, though it lacks the logic which P—Kt5 would have had.

14. P×P ch, K×P; 15. K—Kt4, K—B5. If he had played K—K4, the answer would have been 16. K—B5, P—R4; 17. P—B3 !, P—B4; 18. K—Kt5, K—Q4; 19. P—B4 ch, K—Q5; 20. P—B5, P—R5; 21. P—B6, P—R6;

22. P—B7, P—R7; 23. P—B8 Q, P—R8 (Q); 24. Q—KR8 ch and wins. After the move of the‘text a very similar end would have come, had I not had another attack of "Chess blindness"—Tarrasch called it "amaurosia scacchistica." I continued with 16. K—B5, throwing away the hard-earned win. I should of course have simply advanced my Bishop's Pawn, forcing K—K4. Then 17. K—B5 would have led to the variation just discussed, in which Black loses his Queen. Black now continued with K×P, 17. K—Q5, K—Kt6 and we both queened our Pawns. A long drawn out ending ensued, with Queen against Queen and Pawn, and finally a draw was reached.

End-games in which pieces are left in addition to Pawns are usually easier to handle than pure Pawn endings. They rarely require subtle King maneuvers of the type which in the latter we saw are sometimes decisive. The question most frequently asked is whether in an ending the Knight or the Bishop is preferable. The answer is that this depends almost always on the Pawn position. When there are Pawns on both sides of the board which do not block each other the Bishop is usually stronger because he can move faster from one wing to the other, in support of his advancing Pawns. If the Pawns are blocked the player of the Knight often has the edge, provided he can place his Pawns on squares which are not of the color of the Bishop. The fact that a Bishop controls only squares of one color is a definite drawback due to which a player must often be satisfied with a draw in spite of a Pawn majority. In the position of Diagram 20 which occurred in a game I had with Alekhine (New York 1924) I could not win

because after 1. B—Kt White can sacrifice his Bishop as
soon as my Queen's Pawn, protected by my King, advances. Thereafter I cannot queen my Rook's Pawn because my Bishop is "of the wrong color." The white King
takes refuge on his King's Rook's square and the Bishop
cannot drive him out of it.

DIAGRAM 20.

If the Rook's Pawn, aided by my King, advances to
R7 with a check, White's King will be stalemated unless
Black gives up the protection of the Pawn on the next
move. But with the Bishop alone, of course, the King cannot be mated.

A Knight in place of the Bishop would win easily as
he can obtain control of squares of either color.

A position with the lone Knight worth mentioning because it shows a characteristic strength and weakness
of his is shown in Diagram 21.

If it is White's move he wins with 1. Kt—K2, K—R8;
2. Kt—B1, for Black is forced to deprive his King of his
only flight square by P—R7 whereupon White mates
with 3. Kt—Kt3. But if it is Black's turn to play White

cannot win because he cannot "lose a tempo" with the
Knight, i.e. he cannot reproduce the same position in an
odd number of moves so that it would be his own turn
to play. No matter how many moves the Knight makes,
he will return to the same square always in an even num-

DIAGRAM 21.

ber of moves, so that Black's King will be on R7 instead
of R8 when the Knight reaches B sq.

The Bishop, on the other hand, is often able to lose a
tempo with decisive advantage. Diagram 22 shows a
case in point.

It is White's turn to play. If it were Black's move he
would lose either his Queen's Rook's Pawn or his King
Knight's Pawn as either his King or Knight must move.
White will, therefore, try to reproduce the same position
with Black's turn to play. He does it by moving his
Bishop twice before returning to Q3, thus: 1. B—B1,
K—Kt3; 2. B—K2, K—B3 (or R3); 3. B—Q3. Now
Black is lost because after Kt—B3; 4. B×P, Kt×KtP; 5.
B—Kt7 he must give up his Knight for the advancing
Pawn and White wins the other black Pawns again by

a "tempo" maneuver of his Bishop: 5. . . . ., K—Kt3; 6.
P—R6, Kt×P; 7. B×Kt, K—B3; 8. B—Q3 etc. It is interesting to note that the game would be a draw if

DIAGRAM 22.

White's Pawn were on KR2 instead of KKt2, because the
Bishop would again be of the wrong color, as in the position of Diagram 20.

Tempo maneuvers of a Bishop sometimes decide a
game also against a Bishop of his own color who has to
keep two Pawns protected, as in the example shown in
Diagram 23 in which White has much the better game
not only because his Pawns cannot be attacked while
Black is tied to the protection of his own Pawns, but
also because Black's King cannot move without White's
King advancing and winning either the Bishop's Pawn
or the King's Pawn.

White wins by playing so as to place his Bishop on
B3, attacking both the King's and Rook's Pawns, at a
time when Black's Bishop is on B2, the only square from
which he can protect both Pawns. Forced to move he
must then give up the protection of one of them: 1.

B—K3, B—R2; 2. B—B1 !, B—Kt1; 3. B—Q2, B—B2;
4. B—B3 etc. or 2. . . . ., B—Kt3; 3. B—Kt2, B—B2; 4.
B—B3 etc.

DIAGRAM 23.

Before leaving the subject of Knights and Bishops I
want to call attention to a weakness of the Knight, which
lies in the fact that he can reach a corner from only two
squares and which often prevents him from defending a
position adequately against a passed Rook's Pawn. In
the position of Diagram 24 White has apparently the advantage because Black's Queen's Rook's Pawn is easily
attacked by White and cannot be defended. Also, Black's
Pawns on the King's wing are weak because they cannot
protect each other. On the other hand, though Black's
passed Pawn is lost, he forces White's King away from
the centre so that Black's King can break through there.
White's King side Pawns will then be attacked from the
rear and probably captured while the Knight retaliates
by gobbling up Black's Pawns. Then, in the end, the
Bishop will be able to sacrifice himself for White's passed
Pawn and a draw will be the result.

Endings of this type are usually very tricky and require great care on either side. The position of the diagram is rather typical and a detailed analysis of the possibilities

DIAGRAM 24.

it holds will greatly aid the understanding of the comparative value of Bishop and Knight.

To start with 1. Kt—B5 ch would be a bad blunder as Black would simply exchange the Bishop for the Knight and remain with the "distant passed Pawn" and win. 1. P—Kt5, P—R6; would leave White in a similar difficulty. The best plan appears to be to first play K—B4, restricting the black King. P—R6 could then be answered by 2. K—Kt3, K—Q4; 3. Kt—B4 ch, and after K—Q5; 4. K×P Black cannot approach White's Pawns via K6 as Kt—Q5 ch would win the Bishop. However, the great versatility of the Bishop enables Black to accomplish his purpose after all. He would play B—B2, attacking the Knight, and after 5. P—Kt3 he would continue with B—Q3. Now he threatens K—K6 as well as K—B5, and no matter which one of the threats White defends, Black saves the day because his King is closer to the battle

field. For example: 6. K—R4, K—K6; 7. Kt—Q5 ch,
K×P; 8. Kt×P, K—Kt7; 9. Kt×P, P—B4 ! etc.

Dangerous for Black would be the immediate capture
of White's Pawn, though with best play he could draw
even then. But the slightest misstep would be fatal. For
example: 9. ...., K×P; 10. P—Kt4, K—Kt6; 11.
P—KKt5, K—B5; 12. P—Kt5, K—B4; 13. P—QKt6,
K—Kt3; 14. Kt—B6, B—B5 (K×P ? 15. Kt—K4 ch); 15.
K—Kt5, K×P; 16. Kt—Q5, B—K4 ? The best Black can
do now is produce an ending with Queen against Queen
and Knight, though in an actual game he would probably not find the correct continuation due to the many
trappy maneuvers which are at White's disposal. If he
played B—Kt he would draw, for after 17. K—B6,
P—B4; 18. K—Kt7, B—K4; 19. Kt—B7, P—B5; 20.
K—B6, P—B6; or 17. Kt—B7, P—B4; 18. Kt—R6,
P—B5 ! White obviously has no winning combination.
But after 16. ...., B—K4 White wins an all-important
tempo. Black cannot advance the Pawn when White
plays 17. K—B6, because 18. Kt—B7 would threaten
P—Kt7 and Black could not stop the Pawn with B—Q5
on account of the check on K6. Thus he would have to
move the King to a square where the Knight cannot get
at him. The most plausible move would be 17. ....,
K—Kt5. But this would lose because after 18. Kt—B7,
B—Q5; 19. P—Kt7, B—R2; 20. Kt—Kt5, B—Kt; 21.
K—Q7, P—B4; 22. K—B8, P—B5 (if the Bishop moves
the Knight cuts him off from the queening square); 23.
K×B, P—B6; 24. Kt—B3 ! White stops the Pawn with
Kt—Q and Kt—K3 ch.

Had Black moved his King to R4, the Knight would
have caught the Queen with a check on KKt3; and

K—R3 or K—R5 would have enabled the Knight to reach K3 in time to stop the Pawn via Q4 and B5 ch. The only move at Black's disposal would have been 17. ...., K—Kt3. After 18. K—B6, B—Q5 White must then be satisfied with winning the Bishop. Whether he can win the ensuing ending with Queen and Knight against Queen is problematical.

If on the 6th move White had played Kt—R4 instead of K—R4, the continuation might have been: 6. ...., K—B5; 7. Kt×P, B×P ch; 8. K—R4, B—K2 !; 9. Kt×P, K—Q5; 10. P̣—B4, K—K6; 11. K—Kt5, K—B7; 12. K—B6, K—Kt7; 13. K—Q7, B—Kt5; Now White can no longer hold his Pawns. 14. Kt—B6, for example, is answered with K×P; 15. Kt—Q5, K×P etc.

In the position of Diagram 24 White could try for a win with 1. Kt—Kt2, as luckily for him the reply B—Q5 ch!! turns out to be wrong. After 2. K×B, P—R6 White's King cannot stop the Pawn, for 3. K—B3 would be answered by P—R7. The "excuse" at White's disposal is 3. Kt—Q3, P—R7; 4. Kt—B5 ch and 5. Kt—Kt3. With Black's King on K2 instead of Q3 the Bishop sacrifice would be correct. As it is, Black would have to reply B—Kt8, and after 2. Kt×P, B×P White would have the edge on account of his passed Pawn and Black's inability to attack the King's wing when White places his Knight on K2.

Knight or Bishop fighting against a Rook usually lose the ending if the player of the Rook can obtain a passed Pawn by giving up the Rook for the minor piece. Diagram 25 shows an example which illustrates the typical procedure. White first forces Black's King away from the Pawn which bars the advance of his own Knight's Pawn

and then gives up the Rook for Bishop and Pawn: 1.
R—R7 ch, K—K3; 2. R—B7, P—Kt4; 3. R×P ch, B×R;
4. K×B. It would take Black six moves to queen his

Knight's Pawn while White requires only four moves
to reach the queening square. If Black's King's Bishop's
Pawn had already been advanced to the fourth square
he would now draw, because he would queen one move
after White. However, White would then not have sacrificed the Rook in the manner just shown but he would
have attacked the King's side Pawns instead. The procedure, with Black's Pawn on KB4, might have been:
1. R—R3, B—K5; 2. R—KKt3, P—B5; 3. R—Kt4 etc. or
1. . . . ., B—Q4; 2. P—Kt5, K—B2; 3. R—R6 etc.

If no Pawns are left on the board the Rook can win
against Bishop or Knight only if the defending King
happens to be placed very unfavorably, allowing the
Rook to force him to the edge of the board with the
other King in opposition so that the Rook may either
threaten mate and attack the minor piece at the same
time or pin it and capture it because the King must move

and give up its protection. The position of Diagram 26 illustrates such a case. White wins with 1. K—Q6 which

DIAGRAM 26.

attacks the Bishop and threatens mate. If Black defends the mate with B—B6 White plays R—KB5 again attacking the Bishop and threatening mate, and Black has no reply. Had Black played 1. ....., B—Kt5, White would have won through 2. R—R8ch, B—B; 3. R—Kt8, followed by the capture of the Bishop.

We turn now to the endings which, as pointed out earlier in this chapter, occur most frequently, i.e. endings with Rooks and Pawns. If only one Pawn is left the most important thing to know is that the defending King can hold the game to a draw if he controls the queening square of the Pawn. Diagram 27 shows an example particularly unfavorable for the defending player, because his Rook is not placed in back of the attacking King so that he could always check him as soon as he assumes opposition and thus threatens mate. In answer to 1. K—Q6 Black would play R—Q2 ch !, and after 2. P×R he would be stalemate. If White instead retreats

with the King Black replies R—Q7 or Q8 and now he
can always check the white King from the rear.

DIAGRAM 27.

When both players have Pawns left in addition to the
Rooks the ending often reverts to a type discussed
among the pure Pawn endings. In the position of Diagram 28, for example, White would play 1. R—R2 and
after R—R2; he would continue with 2. K—Q3, threatening to play the King over to the other side and to drive
Black's Rook out of the road of the passed Pawn. This
threat would force the black King to follow suit and in
that way White would finally gain access to Black's
Pawns. The play might proceed as follows: 2. ....,
K—Q4; 3. R—R5 ch, K—Q3; 4. P—R4, K—K3; 5.
P—R5 ! P—Kt4; 6. K—Q4, K—Q3; 7. P—Kt4, and now
White's King will advance either to K5 or to QB5 and
win either Black's Pawns or the Rook. The real reason
why Black cannot hold this ending is the lack of mobility of his Rook. Against a mobile Rook it is sometimes
very difficult to transform a Pawn plus into a win. The
position of Diagram 29 occurred in a tournament game

I had against an opponent who offered me a draw thinking I had no chance to force the advance of my Queen's
Bishop's Pawn. He argued that he could place his Rook
on QB2 and keep checking my King as soon as I tried to
support the advance of the Pawn through K—Q3 or
K—Kt3. If I tried to support the advance with R—QB2,
on the other hand, he would reply K—K6 and attack my
Pawn with both King and Rook. I refused the draw be-

DIAGRAM 28.

cause it occurred to me that if I could lure his King into
a less favorable position, Kt6 for example, from where
he could not readily reach K6, I could first bring up my
King as far as QR4 and then advance my Pawn under
the protection of the Rook without interference by
White's King. If I only had a waiting move after 1. K—
B2; R—QB2, everything would be fine! But I could not
very well move my Rook from his ideal spot where he
protects the Knight's Pawn and at the same time keeps
White's King from cooperating with his Rook. Thus I
had to try to lose a move through a maneuver with my
King, in order to make it White's turn to play. Then he

could not move his Rook away from the Bishop's file
because my Pawn would advance, followed by my King.
Neither could he advance his Queen's Rook's Pawn because that would give my Rook a chance to attack it and
force his own Rook into an unfavorable defensive position. After much analysis I thought of a maneuver that
should do the trick: I would go to B sq and not to B2
when checked in the Queen's file or in the Knight's file!

DIAGRAM 29.

And in reply to R—B2 I would then play K—B2 and it
would be White's move! The trouble was he might not
play R—QB2 at the crucial moment but R—KKt2, for
example, waiting for me to go back to B2 with my King
before returning to B2 himself. But then I could at least
advance my Pawn one step further and guard it with my
Rook from QB2 and for the second time with my King
from Kt3. At any rate, it seemed the only reasonable try,
and in order not to betray my plan I first made a number
of King's moves which appeared aimless: 2. K—Kt3,
R—Kt2 ch; 3. K—B4, R—B2 ch; 4. K—Q3, R—Q2 ch;
5. K—B2, R—QB2; 6. K—Q2, R—Q2 ch; 8. K—B sq

R—Q2. Ah! He was unsuspecting! Or he was too sure that he had a draw! 9. K—B2, K—Kt6; Now I had the position I wanted: 10. K—Kt3, R—Kt2 ch; 11. K—R4, R—QB2; 12. R—QB2 ! K—B5. Too late! 13. P—B4, K—K4; 14. K—Kt5 and the advance of the Pawn can no longer be stopped.

The player with the Pawn minority has usually a much easier time when all Pawns are on the same side of the board. Experience has shown that two against one Pawn or three against two Pawns can rarely win while four against three Pawns usually do, because the King can

DIAGRAM 30.

then advance with the Pawns without being exposed to disturbing checks, the fourth Pawn serving to cover his flank.

In view of the many drawing possibilities in Rook and Pawn endings a player who is a Pawn down in endings with several pieces on each side usually seeks his salvation in the exchange of all pieces but the Rooks. An example is shown in Diagram 30. I had the black pieces in the game in which this position occurred, and I felt

that my best drawing chance lay in exchanging at least
one of the King's side Pawns and preferably also the
Knight and the Queen's side Pawns. Therefore I played
first P—KR4. After 2. P—KR3, P×P; 3. P×P I continued with P—Kt6; 4. P×P, R—Q, threatening Kt×P.
White cannot defend with R—B3 on account of the
check on K7. He played 5. Kt—B and R—Kt; 6. R×P,
Kt×P forced the exchange 7. Kt×Kt, R×Kt. It would
now have been a very bad idea on White's part to try to
hold the Knight's Pawn with R—R2, because R—Kt6 ch
followed by R×P and R back to QKt5 would have kept
the white Rook immobile and would have prevented the
white King from advancing to the centre. White realized this and played 8. K—B2, R×P ch; 9. K—B3,
R—Kt5; 10. R—R8 ch, K—R2; 11. R—KB8. After
R—Kt2 White would not have gained anything through
K—B4 because R—Kt5 ch; K—Kt5, R—K5 would have
won the King's Pawn, the protection R—K8 being in-
effective on account of P—B3 ch ! Thus White tried
12. P—Kt5, overlooking that after P—Kt3; 13. P—B6 I
had a forced draw through perpetual check or stalemate.
This possibility offers itself not infrequently and the
position is therefore worthy of study. The continuation
was R—Kt6 ch; 14. K—K4, R—K6 ch; 15. K—Q5,
R—Q6 ch and now the Rook continues checking up and
down the Queen's file. Even 15. ...., R×P ch would
have forced the draw, for 16. K—Q6, R—K3 ch;
17. K—Q7, R—Q3 ch !; 18. K—K7, R—K3 ch; 19. K×P,
R—K2 ch leads to a stalemate no matter whether White
takes the Rook with the King or with the Pawn.

   In Rook and Pawn endings in which the Pawns are
even but are not located on the same side of the board

it often happens that one of the players will succeed in advancing a passed Pawn to the seventh so that the Rook must sacrifice himself to prevent the Pawn from queening, but that a win cannot be forced because the other player can also force a Pawn of his up and get the opponent's Rook for it. These endings usually require very careful counting of moves to make sure that the hostile King cannot reach the Pawn in time to hold him.

The position of Diagram 31 is rather typical for this

DIAGRAM 31.

kind of ending. White must give up his Rook right away. He cannot play R—K ch because Black's Rook would interpose. Otherwise the check would have the advantage that after capturing the Rook the King would be one line farther away from White's Pawns. After 1. R×P, K×R; White would lose if he advanced his Pawn to R5 immediately rather than carefully figuring out the sequel. 2. P—R5, P×P ch forces 3. K×P and now it takes White five moves to advance his Pawn to Kt7 and his King to R7. But it is Black's turn to play and in five moves he can reach KB2 with his King and have his Rook on B sq, so that he wins the Pawn. White can force a draw with 1. K—Kt5 ! After K—B6; 2. P—R5, P×P; he can now recapture with the Pawn and his King bars the way of the black King to the Pawn: 3. P×P, K—Q5; 4. P—R6, K—K4; 5. P—R7, R—B sq; 6. K—Kt6 etc.

The most innocent looking Rook and Pawn endings will sometimes give rise to astounding combinations. Diagram 32 shows a famous example. At first glance one

DIAGRAM 32.

would think that Black should have no difficulty in drawing with R—Q3 ch, as White cannot move his King into the Bishop's file without enabling the Rook to occupy this file with a check from White's rear, thus controlling the queening square. But after 2. K—Kt5, R—Q4 ch; 3. K—Kt4, R—Q5 ch; 4. K—Kt3, R—Q6 ch White can finally gain the Bishop's file with 5. K—B2 and the Rook cannot get back of the King. However, here comes the first surprise: Black plays R—Q5 and if White queens the Pawn Black checks on B5 and after Q×R Black is stalemate! Alas! This combination, subtle as it is, has unfortunately a big hole. White counters it with a much more surprising one: 6. P—B8 becomes a Rook!! Now mate is threatened on QR8 and Black's only move is R—QR5, whereupon 7. K—Kt3 attacks the Rook and at the same time threatens mate on B sq so that Black is lost.

When both Rooks are still on the board on either side, the player who succeeds in doubling Rooks on his seventh rank frequently obtains a winning advantage either through mating threats or by attacking the Pawns of the opponent from the rear.

In the ending two Rooks, due to the tremendous force they exert when doubled, are usually preferable to the Queen. Even if the player of the Queen is one or two Pawns ahead the game can be drawn by the Rooks who occupy both the same rank and thus prevent the Pawns from passing, provided they are separated so that they cannot protect each other's advance.

Strategic Principles

O EVERY BEGINNER there seems to be a bewildering choice of moves each time it is his turn to play. To analyze step by step the consequences of each possible move would obviously take more time than anyone would care to spend on such a task even if it could be accomplished. There must be a short cut enabling a player to narrow that choice by selecting just a few moves which are *likely* to yield an advantage and rejecting all others as unlikely to do so. Such a short cut is offered only by the understanding how to evaluate a move from general principles rather than from detailed analysis.

This does not mean that it will always be possible to conclude definitely that one move is better than another. The final choice will often depend upon the temperament of the player. One might prefer an attacking move,

another a defensive one. But the finer the understanding
of the general strategic laws the smaller will be the number of moves a player will take under consideration.
There is again a striking parallel in music. A student
whose understanding and experience is as yet limited
might think of a half a dozen different ways of render-
ing a composition. To the accomplished musician there
will be only one—not necessarily the one the composer
himself had in mind, but probably one very close to it,
individual style accounting for deviations.

The general laws of Chess strategy are surprisingly
simple and few in number. In fact, they can almost be
reduced to one single principle which might be termed
the principle of mobility.

After all, Chessmen differ in strength from each other
not because they have different shapes but because one
can control more squares at a time than another. In the
original set-up of the pieces their potential force can
obviously not be utilized. They have not the mobility
which they would have if their lines of action were not
blocked by Pawns and by each other, and it is only reasonable to assume that the player who places his pieces
so that they have more mobility than those of his opponent will have an advantage of position. In the language
of physics we might say he has stored in his pieces more
potential energy so that he will be able to get more work
done by them than his adversary.

Let us see how we can apply this principle to the
opening of the game. In deciding where to place the
Knights we have no difficulty at all. Evidently they will
be placed very well on B3 because from there they have
more squares to go to than from any other square they

could reach in one move. In the case of the Bishops the decision is not as easy. First of all it requires some Pawn moves to get them out. But which Pawns should we move for the purpose? The Knight's Pawns or the King's and Queen's Pawns? Very likely it is not the best plan to move a Knight's Pawn to start with, because only one piece would be freed in this way while advancing the King's or Queen's Pawn opens a path for both Bishop and Queen and also an additional square for one of the Knights. It is true that sometimes a Bishop finds more work to do in the long diagonal than in any other line. But that depends upon the formation the opponent chooses for his Pawns, and we will discuss this point in due course.

What I want to stress at the outset is that the first eight or ten moves in any game should normally serve no other aim but to increase the mobility of *all* pieces and that one piece must not be singled out for this purpose to the detriment of others. This is what beginners always fail to consider. After a game has been started with 1. P—K4, P—K4; 2. Kt—KB3, for example, beginners will look at this Knight's move only from the point of view that it attacks the King's Pawn. In reality this is no argument in favor of that move since the King's Pawn can be defended without any difficulty through QKt—B3 which at the same time develops Black's Knight to a square where his mobility is much improved. The fact that White's Knight can reach no other square with his first move on which his mobility would be greater than on B3 is a perfectly sufficient reason to select the move. On K2 he would have the same mobility, but he would obstruct Queen and King's Bishop.

After 2. ...., Kt—QB3 beginners will usually look
for immediate further activity for the Knight just developed. Seeing that he cannot go to KKt5 from where he
attacks Black's King's Bishop's Pawn and King's Rook's
Pawn, because the Queen could capture him there,
White will play 3. P—Q3 or P—KR4 in order to then
follow up with Kt—Kt5. Such a plan should be recog-

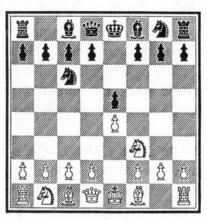

DIAGRAM 33.

nized as bad without any further investigation, because
it does not consider the mobility of the other pieces.
P—Q3 would be opening a line for the Queen's Bishop
but at the same time it would be restricting the King's
Bishop. Therefore that move should be postponed until
the King's Bishop is out. P—KR4 increases the mobility
of the King's Rook, but again without consideration of
the other pieces. Planning to play the Rook out to R3
and from there over to the centre or the Queen's wing
is obviously futile, as Black, by advancing his Queen's
Pawn, would control White's KR3 with his Queen's
Bishop. The only work the Rook could do in the Rook's
file is aiding the advance of the Rook's Pawn or attack-

ing the black King after he has castled and an opportunity arises to get rid of the Rook's Pawn so that the Rook's file is opened. There is no such opportunity in view, and preparing the advance Kt—Kt5 is altogether premature anyway because an attack with one man cannot possibly be successful unless the adversary makes a bad blunder. There is no square in a player's camp at the beginning which cannot be protected by a move that at the same time develops a piece. An attack has sense only if it can be carried out with more men than the opponent can gather for defense. This is more or less self-evident.

On his third turn White should consider only a move with his Bishop or Kt—QB3. For the Bishop only B4 or Kt5 can be advantageous squares at this stage of the game, for on Q3 he would be obstructing the Queen's Pawn and with it the Queen's Bishop, and on K2 he would be taking away a square from the Queen and he would have less squares to go to than from B4 or Kt5.

On B4 the Bishop attacks Black's KB2, but again this is not the main thing to consider when weighing the advantages of that move as compared with B—Kt5. On Kt5 the Bishop attacks the King's Pawn indirectly, because the latter is at the moment only protected by the Knight for which the Bishop could exchange himself. However, there is no reason to assume that Black should not be able to defend the King's Pawn satisfactorily. In fact, judging from our principle of mobility, the plan just indicated for White is probably downright bad, because the exchange would open lines for Black's Queen and Queen's Bishop and the capture of the King's Pawn would add nothing to White's development. He would

have to look only one move further to realize that Black
would regain the Pawn immediately with Q—Q5.

The point of view from which to compare the moves
B—B4 and B—Kt5 is not the fleeting effect the Bishop
might have in an immediate combination but the more
permanent value White might derive from the pressure
the Bishop will exert either in the diagonal QR2—KKt8
or in the diagonal QR4—K8. This is a question which
general strategic laws cannot answer very definitely. All
we can say is that probably in either diagonal the Bishop
will have a good opportunity to cooperate with other
pieces, because his line of influence reaches well into the
enemy's territory. A little later we shall see that on Kt5,
where the Bishop would be pinning the black Knight as
soon as Black's Queen's Pawn moves, he is liable to be
more effective because he would aid the attack on
Black's centre with P—Q4.

Should White decide on 3. B—B4, Black will consider
no reply other than B—B4 or Kt—B3. There would be
no sense in Black's playing B—Kt5 as White could obstruct the diagonal with P—B3. Black does probably
best to play B—B4 rather than Kt—B3, because the
latter move would invite 4. Kt—Kt5 and the King's
Bishop's Pawn can then be defended only through
P—Q4 with extremely difficult play the outcome of
which is still a matter of controversy among experts.
After 3. . . . ., B—B4; 4. P—Q3 or O—O, Kt—B3 the
move 5. Kt—Kt5 would be entirely uncalled for because
O—O would protect the Pawn for the second time and
the Knight will be forced to retreat very soon. Thus
White would be losing valuable time which he could
have employed in bringing more forces into play.

It is a very good plan to make it a rule to develop a different piece with every move no matter how tempting a diversion may seem which involves a second move with the same piece in the opening stage. Naturally, this rule must not be taken too literally. If your opponent makes bad moves in the opening, i.e. moves which do not develop his forces rapidly, you may see an opportunity for an early kill through a violent attack, or at least for an attack which will yield some advantage in material, even before you have completed your own development.

Suppose Black answers White's move 4. O—O with Kt—K2, leading to the position shown in Diagram 34.

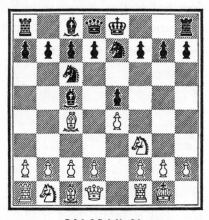

DIAGRAM 34.

This would justify the excursion 5. Kt—Kt5 because the black Knight does not protect the Rook's Pawn which we saw in the second chapter often forms a welcome target for an attack after the King has castled. 5. ....., O—O would now be followed by 6. Q—R5 which attacks both the Rook's and the Bishop's Pawn, and after P—R3; 7. Kt×P Black must give up the Rook for the

Knight to avoid the disastrous discovered check Kt—Q6.

Generally only two Pawn moves are needed in the opening, one with the King's Pawn and one with the Queen's Pawn, to develop all pieces with the exception of the Rooks. In King's Pawn openings in which both players have advanced their Pawn to K4 it is always a good plan for White to play P—Q4 rather than Q3, because on Q4 the Pawn attacks K5 and usually forces the exchange of these two Pawns sooner or later. The result then is the Pawn skeleton shown in Diagram 35 which, other things being equal, holds more promises for White. The reason is that White retains a Pawn in the centre and thus controls one of Black's centre squares (Q4) while Black does not control a square in White's centre. The squares KB4 and QB4 are next in importance to the

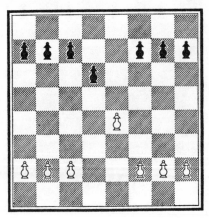

DIAGRAM 35.

centre squares, and again White's centre Pawn controls one of them while Black does not have equivalent control. The only advantage this Pawn position holds for Black is that White's King's Pawn offers a target for Black's Rooks which might be placed in the King's file, while the only open file White's Rooks have is effectively blocked by Black's Queen's Pawn as long as the latter remains protected by the Bishop's Pawn.

In games opened with P—Q4 by both players the two centre files often remain closed because the King's Pawn

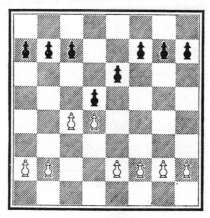

DIAGRAM 36.

cannot ordinarily be advanced to the fourth square without considerable preparation. In such games it is imperative that another file be opened for the Rooks to work in. Sometimes an opportunity arises to advance the King's Bishop's Pawn after playing the King's Knight to K5. But more often the Rooks aim at control of the Queen's Bishop's file, and with this object in mind the Queen's Bishop's Pawn is advanced to the fourth at an early stage, leading to the skeletons shown in Diagrams 36 or 37. In Diagram 37 we note that Black has moved the King's Knight's Pawn instead of the King's Pawn. The plan is, of course, to exert pressure with the Bishop from Kt2 on White's centre Pawn. If Black plays his Queen's Bishop's Pawn only to the third thus supporting his Queen's Pawn solidly, he is liable thereby to keep his Queen's Bishop shut in for a long time. This Bishop often finds a good field of activity in the long diagonal, usually on QKt2, and on QB3 the Pawn would obstruct the Bishop.

DIAGRAM 37.

The fight for the control of centre squares has a very obvious reason if we relate it to our leading principle of mobility. From a centre square a piece exerts an influence on either wing. Also, it controls squares in the enemy's territory and for that reason alone is very annoying. The player who controls the centre has almost always more territory at his disposal within which to shift his pieces around quickly according to the demands of the situation. Usually, with his minor pieces placed in the fourth and fifth rank, he has the third rank available for operations with a Rook, swinging him either to the King's or the Queen's wing via Q3 or K3, while the minor pieces of the opponent are confined to the second and third ranks and make rapid shifts of the Rooks difficult.

In modern Chess Black is rarely seen replying to White's P—K4 or P—Q4 with the same move. The idea is not to place this Pawn target in the centre until sufficient preparations have been made to hold it there rather than exchange it under conditions which afford White more freedom of movement. In answer to 1. P—K4 one of the favorite replies is today P—QB4 (Sicilian defense). Black will exchange this Pawn against White's advancing Queen's Pawn and thus obtain an open file for his Rooks. Also, he retains both of his centre Pawns and later on will be able to use them to contest control of the centre squares. In answer to 1. P—Q4 Black usually plays first Kt—KB3 and takes up either the Pawn position shown in Diagram 37 or he continues with P—K3 and later advances the Queen's Pawn to the fourth.

If Black plays P—K3 in answer to P—Q4 on the first move, White can switch into a King's Pawn opening with 2. P—K4. The reply P—Q4 (French defense) will then frequently lead to the Pawn skeleton shown in Diagram 38. Here it is really Black who obtains pressure against centre squares. His QB Pawn is already in place for this purpose and his KB Pawn will advance to the third at the first opportunity, attacking White's King's Pawn. White's compensation for the pressure Black has on the centre lies in his greater freedom of action on the King's wing, where he has much more territory available than Black. After castling he might advance his KB Pawn and thus find useful employment for his Rooks before Black can operate with his Rooks effectively in the QB file.

In positions in which the centre files are blocked— usually through the advance to the fifth rank of either White's King's or Queen's Pawn—White will as a rule obtain more territory on one wing and Black on the

other, and consequently the players will attack on different sides of the board. Naturally the attack against the
King's position is always more dangerous. But the player
who withstands the attack against his King often obtains
a decisive advantage on the other wing because his opponent has concentrated most of his forces in the attack

DIAGRAM 38.

and cannot reorganize them rapidly enough for defense
on a distant battle field.

The Pawn skeletons discussed above will, of course,
undergo changes as the game progresses. But these
changes should never be undertaken in the opening or
in the early middle-game unless they fit harmoniously
into the scheme of development dictated by the great
principle of mobility. In other words, in the opening no
Pawn move should be made which does not add something to the mobility of a piece, and in the early middle-
game only such Pawn moves should be considered which
aid maneuvers aiming at control of centre squares. In
the later middle-game, when attacks are executed, the
Pawn skeleton often loses its characteristic form as a

whole wing advances. But it is not rare to see it pre-
served almost into the very ending.

A few examples will illustrate the characteristics of
good and bad Pawn moves.

The position of Diagram 39 may be reached after
1. P—K4, P—K4; 2. P—Q4, P×P; 3. Q×P. A beginner

DIAGRAM 39.

might be tempted here to continue with P—QB4, driv-
ing the Queen away. This would be a Pawn move en-
tirely contrary to the exigencies of a position in which
White has an open Queen's file. Unless Black's Queen's
Pawn can force the advance to Q4 the Queen's Bishop's
Pawn is needed on B2 to protect the Queen's Pawn on
Q3 in case of pressure in the Queen's file by White's
Rooks.

Diagram 40 illustrates a similar theme. This position
would be reached after 1. P—K4, P—Q4; 2. P×P,
Kt—KB3. White should not let himself be tempted to
hold the Pawn he has just captured by continuing
3. P—QB4, P—B3; 4. P×P. For after Kt×P Black would
obtain complete control of White's centre square Q4,

for example through 5. Kt—KB3, P—K4 followed by
B—QB4, and White's Queen's Pawn will then remain
"backward" on Q3, exposed to the attack of the black
Rooks in the Queen's file. The argument that Black
would finally only regain the Pawn he has sacrificed in
the opening does not hold, as Black emerges from the

DIAGRAM 40.

opening with the control of the centre and with it—as
always in such a case—much greater mobility for his
pieces.

If White does play 3. P—QB4—and there is no objection to such a move as it attacks one of the centre
squares of the opponent—he must see to it that he keeps
control of his own centre squares and avoids a backward
Pawn. He would continue 3. . . . ., P—B3; 4. P—Q4 !,
P×P; 5. Kt—B3, thus turning the game into some sort
of a Queen's Pawn opening, characterized by the Pawn
skeleton shown in Diagram 36, which might have under-
gone a very natural change by Black advancing his
Queen's Bishop's Pawn and exchanging it after White's
P—K3.

The position of Diagram 41 occurred in a game I had against Tartakower in New York, 1924, after the opening moves 1. P—K4, P—K4; 2. Kt—KB3, Kt—QB3; 3. P—Q4, P×P; 4. Kt×P, Kt—B3; (Scotch game) 5. Kt×Kt, KtP×Kt; 6. Kt—Q2, B—B4. Tartakower's bizarre manner of opening the game certainly cannot be good for White. In exchanging the Knights he has doubled my Pawns in the QB file but while this would be a disadvantage in a Rook ending it is likely to turn into an advantage in the middle game. First of all the Pawn on QB3 controls a centre square and secondly there is always an open file for a Rook where a Pawn has been doubled. From Q2 the Knight intends to go to Kt3, but the King's Pawn is loose, and if White played

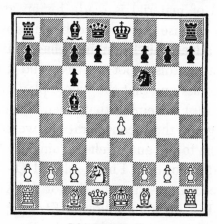

DIAGRAM 41.

7. B—Q3 the consequence would be P—Q4, again attacking the King's Pawn. Exchanging on Q5 would leave Black with a strong centre Pawn and undouble his Pawns. Advancing to K5, on the other hand, would give Black an immediate winning attack, similar to that illustrated in Diagram 34. He would proceed as follows:

8. P—K5, Kt—Kt5; 9. O—O, Q—R5; 10. P—KR3, Kt×P;
11. R×Kt, B×R ch; etc. (12. K—R2 ?, B×P ! and mate
in a few moves).

In the position of Diagram 41 Tartakower played
1. P—K5. This advance of the King's Pawn to the fifth is
always a very dubious procedure. For one thing the
move relinquishes one of the main advantages of a
centre Pawn on the fourth rank, that of controlling two
important squares on the fifth rank. Then, the farther a
Pawn advances the more easily the opponent can attack
him and force his exchange which will often open a file
for a hostile Rook.

The advance of the King's Pawn to the fifth rank
usually entails an advantage only in positions in which
a good deal of material is ready for an attack on the
King whose defense is weakened by the absence of the
Knight the advancing Pawn has chased away. In the
present situation this is not the case, and it is therefore
reasonable to assume that the whole plan initiated with
Kt—Q2 is bad. I remember that when I faced this situation in the game these considerations were a source of
much comfort to me and I felt certain that I would obtain the better position. First I played Q—K2, forcing
White's Queen to obstruct the line of the King's Bishop
with 2. Q—K2, and then followed Kt—Q4; 3. Kt—Kt3,
B—Kt3. In this position, shown in Diagram 42, the
strategic plans which will govern White's and Black's
play in the middle game are these: White will castle on
the Queen's side because in that way he will get a Rook
more quickly into the centre. Also, he will try to maintain
his Pawn on K5 if possible, perhaps with P—KB4, B—Q2
and—after driving the Knight from Q5—with B—B3.

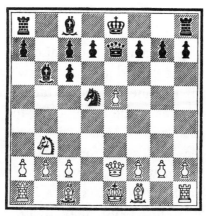

DIAGRAM 42.

Black will castle on the King's side and play P—B3 in order to open the King's Bishop's file for the Rook, and he will attack on the Queen's side with P—QR4, provoking P—QR4 on White's part also, which would weaken the protective chain of Pawns in front of White's King.

This brings us to a most important subject, the discussion of changes in the Pawn skeleton on the side on which the King has castled. Generally speaking one might say that Pawn moves on that side usually produce a weakness and should only be made either when forced by a direct threat of the opponent or when they form part of an attacking maneuver. The latter would imply that the player in question has the superior mobility on that wing and need not fear invasion by his adversary's forces.

The weakness entailed in any Pawn move is that the square protected by the Pawn in his initial position loses that protection after the Pawn has moved and can never enjoy it again because a Pawn cannot move backward. Thus, moving the Knight's Pawn in front of the King

weakens the squares B3 and R3, and we have seen the
disastrous effects of such weaknesses in the chapter in
which mating combinations were discussed.

Another weakness produced by a Pawn move is that
the Pawn itself becomes an easier target for attack by
the opposing Pawns in the neighboring files. Usually an
exchange against one of these neighboring Pawns will
secure an open Rook's file for the adversary. Against
the Knight's Pawn who has advanced to the third, the
opponent is liable to run his Rook's Pawn to the fifth.
P—R3, on the other hand, may invite the opposing
Knight's Pawn up to Kt5.

After P—R3 the square Kt3 is usually still covered
by the Bishop's Pawn. But if the latter also moves up, a
"hole" is produced on Kt3 which the opponent may occupy with one of his pieces. The move P—KR3 has perhaps lost more games for the average player at an early
stage than any other. On R3 the Pawn is usually attacked
by the opponent's Queen's Bishop and not infrequently
the sacrifice of the Bishop for the Pawn opens the
Knight's file for a winning attack of Rook and Queen,
particularly when the adversary's Knight is posted on
his KB5 from where he controls the squares Kt7 and R6.

Diagrams 43 and 44 show two typical positions in
which the possibility of such sacrificial combinations has
to be investigated before advancing the Rook's Pawn or
both the Rook's and Knight's Pawns.

In the position of Diagram 43 White has just played
B—KKt5, threatening Kt—Q5 with continuations similar
to those discussed in connection with Diagram 6. The
proper defense is 1. ...., B—K3, in order to exchange
the Knight should he go to Q5. Beginners usually try to

defend themselves by chasing away the Bishop with
1. ...., P—KR3; 2. B—R4, P—KKt4. But then White
can work up a terrific attack by first sacrificing the
Knight and then bringing up more forces against the

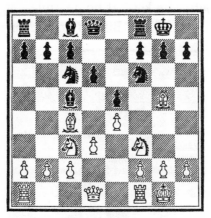

DIAGRAM 43.

pinned King's Knight: 3. Kt×P, P×Kt; 4. B×P. Again
Kt—Q5 is threatened and this time Black is forced to
make the move he should have chosen in the first instance. 4. ...., B—K3. White will then perhaps continue
either with K—R, in order to be able to play P—KB4 and
bring the Rook to bear on Black's King's Knight, or he
will prepare the advance of the Bishop's Pawn with
Kt—QR4 and the exchange of Black's King's Bishop.

In the position of Diagram 44, in which Black
threatens B×Kt followed by Q×P mate, White would
do best defending himself with KR—B, for after
1. P—KR3 he would be exposed to a powerful attack
commencing with B×P; 2. P×B, Q×P, threatening perhaps P—KR4 followed by R—R3, and if B×R, P×B and
a deadly check in the Knight's file. The refusal of the sacrifice with 2. Kt—K5 would offer better chances.

The weakening of squares through moves of Rook's or Knight's Pawn on the side on which the King has not castled is, of course, much less serious than in front of the King, but even there the rule applies that these Pawns had better be kept at home, unless it is necessary to provide a spot for the Bishop on Kt2 or an opposing

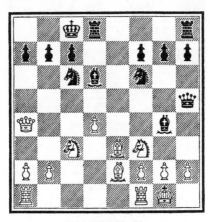

DIAGRAM 44.

Bishop has to be chased with P—R3 and P—Kt4 to unpin a Knight.

The Ruy Lopez, one of the openings used most frequently, offers a good opportunity of discussing the considerations which might be applied in judging whether such Pawn moves fit into the strategic scheme of the game or not.

After 1. P—K4, P—K4; 2. Kt—KB3, Kt—QB3; 3. B—Kt5 the move P—QR3 is not unreasonable, because Black can later intercept the Bishop's line of influence through P—QKt4 in case he needs his Knight to control his squares K4 and Q5. 4. B—R4, Kt—B3; 5. O—O, B—K2 then lead to the position shown in Diagram 45. Black could have captured the King's Pawn on his last move, but this would have invited an attack on his uncastled King with R—K or first P—Q4, and closing the King's file first with B—K2 was therefore probably better.

White could now protect his King's Pawn with Kt—B3 or P—Q3 or Q—K2 or R—K. Only the latter

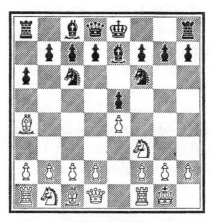

DIAGRAM 45.

two moves should be considered. The strategic plan of the opening is an attack on Black's centre, and for this end the Queen's Pawn should advance to Q4 as soon as feasible. Kt—B3 would give Black an opportunity to exchange White's powerful Bishop with P—QKt4, P—Q3 and Kt—QR4. Most reasonable looks 6. R—K, because the Rook is likely to find a good field of activity in the King's file in case P—Q4 should lead to the exchange of Black's King's Pawn on White's Q4. Now the threat is B×Kt followed by Kt×P and Black must either protect the Pawn with P—Q3 or play P—QKt4.

Here the advance of the Knight's Pawn has several good arguments in its favor. First of all P—Q3 would not have maintained the Black centre Pawn, because

White could have forced its exchange on Q4 after B×Kt.
Secondly, after 7. B—Kt3, P—Q3 White is still unable
to advance his Queen's Pawn to the fourth without getting his good Bishop exchanged. For if 8. P—Q4, Kt×P;
9. Kt×Kt, P×Kt; 10. Q×P ?, Black would win a piece
through P—B4 and P—B5. White would therefore either
have to play B—Q5 before recapturing on Q4 or he
would have to play 10. P—QR4, R—QKt; 11. P×P,
P×P; and then capture on Q4, which does not look so
good either because Black keeps the white Bishop out of
play for a long time with P—B4 and P—B5. For these
reasons White will prepare the advance of the Queen's
Pawn with 8. P—B3, incidentally saving his Bishop
thereby from the exchange through Kt—QR4.

If Black now castles the position of Diagram 46 is
reached. Here we have one of the rare exceptions in

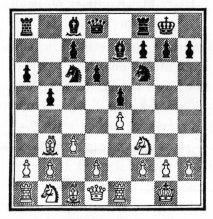

DIAGRAM 46.

which the move P—KR3, to prevent the pin B—Kt5, has
really a logical basis. The white Knight is an important
factor in the struggle for the centre. If White played
P—Q4 right away, B—Kt5 would exert an undesirable

pressure on White's Q4. Another good argument in favor of 9. P—KR3 is the fact that Black has no good square for his Queen's Bishop. To place him on Kt2 would be of doubtful value because the Bishop has much less mobility in the long diagonal in this position than in the line QB—KR6. Besides, in King's Pawn openings the Queen's Bishop is very often needed to control the square KB4 on which otherwise one of the opponent's Knights might profitably take his stand sooner or later. White need not fear that on R3 the Pawn will be a target for a successful attack because Black cannot assemble enough pieces on the King's wing. After 9. ...., B—Q2; 10. P—Q4, Q—B for example, with the same sacrifice in view which we saw succeed in the position of Diagram 44, White would calmly continue with the development of his pieces. 11. QKt—Q2, B×P; 12. P×B, Q×P; 13. Kt—B would leave Black without a satisfactory continuation.

Neither can Black take advantage of the advance of White's Rook's Pawn by storming forward with his Pawns (P—R3, P—R4, P—KKt5, etc.) because his own King would be exposed worse by such a maneuver than White's who would still have two Pawns in front of him for protection.

If Black had not yet castled, White would have to think twice before playing P—KR3, for then the advance of Black's Knight's Pawn would be liable to open a file for Black's Rook.

In the position of the diagram it is customary for Black to seek the initiative on the Queen's wing through Kt—QR4 and P—B4, which maintains the Pawn centre and gains a little elbow room for the minor pieces. We shall encounter this maneuver in some of our sample games later on.

Before leaving the subject of Pawn moves other than absolutely essential for the development of the pieces we must examine what role the Bishops' Pawns play in

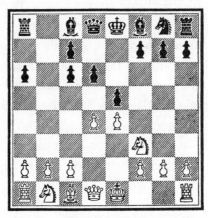

DIAGRAM 47.

the changes the original Pawn skeleton might reasonably undergo in the early middle-game.

We have already seen how the Queen's Bishop's Pawn may profitably be used on B3 to support the Queen's Pawn on Q4, or on B4 to open the Bishop's file for the Rooks. The King's Bishop's Pawn has occasion to serve quite similarly, not only to open the Bishop's file for the Rook by advancing to the fourth, but also on B3, to support the King's Pawn on K4. In the case of the advance of the King's Bishop's Pawn, however, it is important that the diagonal QR2—KKt8 is not liable to get into possession of the adversary's Bishop, as this usually entails a dangerous attack on the King.

In the Ruy Lopez opening just discussed, for instance, such considerations would apply if after 1. P—K4,

P—K4; 2. Kt—KB3, Kt—QB3; 3. B—Kt5, P—QR3;
4. B—R4 Black played P—Q3 and White answered this
with 5. B×Kt, P×B; 6. P—Q4, in order to induce the
exchange of Black's centre Pawn. In this position, pic-
tured in Diagram 47, there would be no objection to
Black's playing P—B3, from the point of view of squares
weakened by this advance, because the opponent's
white Bishop is gone so that no annoyance need be
feared in the diagonal leading to the future residence of
the black King. A valid objection to the move might be
the fact that B3 is the logical square for the Knight and
that its obstruction will delay the development of Black's
King wing.

In the position of Diagram 48, which I faced against
Alekhine in an exhibition game at Paris in 1913, I had

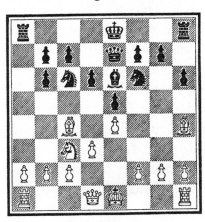

DIAGRAM 48.

just played Q—K2, with the intention of advancing the
King's side Pawns (P—KKt4, P—KR4 etc.) in case
White should castle. Alekhine played much better 1.
P—B3, providing a retreat for his Bishop and planning
the advance P—KKt4 etc. himself in reply to my castling

on the King's side. This induced me to castle on the Queen's side. But in view of the fact that White can open the Queen's Rook's file by exchanging his Rook's Pawn against my Pawn on QKt3 it was likely that the white attack would mature more quickly than the attack I might develop on the King's side. The proper strategy would have been for me to let White castle first and then follow suit on the same wing. Meanwhile I might have prepared the advance P—Q4 with Kt—QR4 or R—Q or both.

In the course of the foregoing discussions of different often recurring Pawn formations we have had occasion to observe also the customary placement of minor pieces and Rooks. While it was mainly through experience and analysis of generations of masters that the most favorable line-up of the pieces has gradually been worked out, considerations of quite general character can again point the right way, without the necessity of laborious memorizing of analyzed variations.

It is evident that in the early part of the game the Rooks should be kept back because the middle of the board is generally controlled by the minor pieces, and it would only lead to loss of time if a Rook ventured out and permitted himself to be driven all over the board by Bishops and Knights. The same consideration holds for the Queen.

When it comes to the question whether to settle a Knight or a Bishop on a centre square we will usually decide in favor of the Knight because we rarely mind the Knight being exchanged against a Bishop while we like to preserve our Bishops and therefore hesitate to expose them to the exchange by a Knight.

After most of the minor pieces are gone the Rooks have much more freedom to engage actively in hand to hand fighting. It is imperative that files are opened for them through the exchange of Pawns. Doubled Rooks in an open file are particularly dangerous on account of their threat to force an entry into the seventh rank in which they often raise havoc among the Pawns.

Let us now practice the application of these general considerations by carefully going through a few games from beginning to end.

Practical Applications

HE FOLLOWING GAME
was not a tournament game but a so called "five minute"
game, i.e. a game played with clocks as fast or as slowly
as the players like, but with the condition that neither
player must exceed the total time of the other by more
than five minutes at any stage.

This manner of timing was very popular in the City of
London Chess Club where this game was played in 1911.
I have some sort of a sentimental attachment to it, not
only because it is the most beautiful game I ever succeeded in winning, but because it was the first game I
played in England, on the day I arrived there, sea sick
from an awful channel crossing, and without knowing a
word of English.

As always when I find myself in a foreign country, my
first visit was to the leading Chess Club, where a Chess

player is sure to find friendly advice. I was introduced to many members whose names I did not understand, and one of them invited me to play a game with him. At that time I was quite unaware that he was Sir George Thomas, the champion of the Club and later British Champion. I was explained the rules of these five minute games by a German speaking member, and we began:

WHITE: *Edward Lasker* BLACK: *Sir George Thomas*

    1. P—Q4   **P—KB4**

The Dutch defense. The move aims at control of White's K4, and possibly at an open file for the King's Rook after castling, in case White should exchange his King's Pawn on K4. A disadvantage which might outweigh these two advantageous features is the fact that Black will have to make at least three Pawn moves to get his pieces developed, since his Queen's Bishop will find no employment except on QKt2 as long as the King's Bishop's Pawn blocks his way.

    2. Kt—KB3   **P—K3**
    3. Kt—QB3

This cannot be a good move at this stage, because Black could now play P—Q4, thoroughly securing his control of my K4. I should first have played P—QB4. If then P—Q4, I can exert pressure against that Pawn with Kt—B3 and possibly with my King's Bishop from Kt2.

    3. ....   **Kt—KB3**

Black does not take advantage of my mistake. Evidently he likes the normal line-up of Pawns and pieces in this opening in which the Queen's Pawn is usually held back to keep the long diagonal open for the Queen's Bishop.

4. B—Kt5

Planning the advance of the King's Pawn.

4. . . . .   B—K2.

Now I must first exchange on KB6 to force the square K4.

5. B×Kt   B×B
6. P—K4   P×P

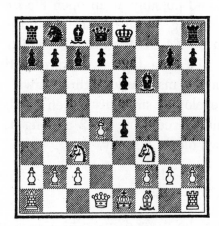

DIAGRAM 49.

Black has nothing better than exchanging this Pawn because if he tried P—QB4, for example, I could advance P—K5 and then P—Q5. In any case, the exchange is in the spirit of the opening.

7. Kt×P   P—QKt3
8. B—Q3   B—Kt2
9. Kt—K5

In view of the fact that I was two moves ahead in the development I felt I could make a second move with this Knight rather than continue in a stereotyped manner with O—O. The Knight, moreover, occupies a centre square and the immediate threat is Q—R5 ch, winning two Pawns, as P—Kt3 would be answered with the Knight sacrifice on Kt6 after which the Bishop falls.

9. ....   O—O
10. Q—R5

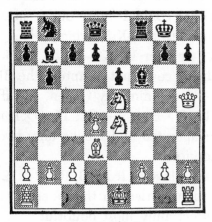

DIAGRAM 50.

As usual, the absence of the protecting King's Knight makes the Rook's Pawn the target of an attack. Checkmate is threatened through Kt×B followed by Q×P. With four pieces on his neck Black has no easy time in finding a satisfactory defense. Obviously he cannot exchange my Queen's Knight as in recapturing I would be attacking his Rook and at the same time threaten again mate on KR7. Neither can he play P—Kt3, as I would give up the Knight for the two Pawns, thus denuding the King and laying him open to all sorts of violent attacks.

If Black interposes his Bishop on KKt2, a simple way for
White to attack would be with P—KR4, for example,
threatening R—R3 and R—Kt3 or possibly the further
advance of the Rook's Pawn.

As we played rather rapidly—we had not used more
than about ten minutes each up to now—my opponent
could not devote very much time to the analysis. I was
not at all sure whether I could keep my attack alive if he
played B×KKt. 11. P×B he could then answer with R—
B4, and 12. Kt—B6 ch would then fail on account of
Q×Kt !! Neither could I figure out a satisfactory continuation after 11. Kt—Kt5, which Black could meet
with P—KR3, or after 11. Kt—B6 ch, R×Kt; 12. Q×P
ch, K—B. Then I could not recapture the Bishop on account of R—R3, winning my Queen, and if 13. Q—R8
ch, K—K2; 14. Q×P ch, R—B2; 15. Q×B my attack is
completely evaporated and I have only two Pawns for
the piece sacrificed.

I would have played 11. P×B, R—B4; 12. Q—Kt4 or
Q—K2 and than castled on the Queen's side, but the
outcome was certainly most doubtful.

Black relieved me of all further worry in this respect
by playing a move I had not expected at all. He continued with

10. ....   Q—K2

intending to recapture with the Knight's Pawn if I should
play Kt×B ch, after which the mate would be defended
by his Queen.

The double attack on KR7, veiled only by my Knight
on K4, suggests, of course, various ways of sacrificing
that Knight in order to open the line of the Bishop. I

had five minutes within which to make up my mind. I was sure that this was the decisive moment of the game, because I cannot bring up more fighting forces in less than three moves, and Black threatens to drive me back by Kt—B3 or P—KKt3 or P—Q3, and then to start operations in the open Bishop's file. Sacrificing my Knight on Kt6, after Black's Knight's Pawn has advanced, would no longer be effective, as Bishop or Queen can interpose on Kt7. For all these reasons I must act immediately and drastically.

The Knight moves which suggest themselves are Kt—Q6 and Kt—Kt5. Both I dismissed after a minute's thought, because after 11. Kt—Kt5, P—Kt3, 12. B×P, P×B; 13. Kt×P, Q—Kt2; 14. Kt×R, K×Kt (Diagram 51) no attack is left, and while two Pawns and a Rook are usually a sufficient equivalent for two minor pieces

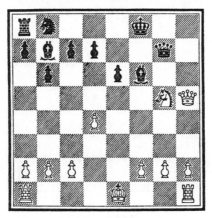

DIAGRAM 51.

in an ending, they rarely are in the middle-game, where due to the superior fighting power of two pieces against one the Pawns are often regained before long.

For this reason Black would avoid exchanging Queens

in this position. After 15. Kt—R7 ch, K—K2; 16. Kt×B, Q×Kt; 17. Q—R7 ch, for example, Black would not interpose the Queen. That would allow the exchange and produce an ending in which the two connected passed Pawns of White would develop into quite a powerful threat. He would, instead answer 17. . . . ., K—Q3, with the intention of playing Kt—R3 and R—KR, whereupon the King could return to the second rank for safety.

The other excursion of the King's Knight which had to be considered in the position of Diagram 50 after Q—K2, Kt—Q6, proves not playable at all, since after P—Kt3; 12. Kt×P, P×Kt; 13. Q×P ch, Q—Kt2; 14. Kt×B Black will exchange Queens, play P—QR4, and then win the Knight with R—R2.

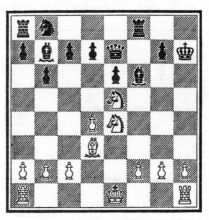

DIAGRAM 52.

After realizing that the preparation by a Knight's move was too slow to make my attack succeed, it occurred to me that I could possibly sacrifice the Queen, forcing the King into the line of my Bishop, and then discover a check with disastrous effect. Diagram 52 shows the position reached after the sacrifice. I saw right away, not without a flush of excitement, that Black would indeed be checkmate if after 12. Kt×B double ch the King went back to R sq. 13. Kt—Kt6 would do the trick. But what if he moved out to R3? Well, a check with my King's Knight on Kt4 would leave him only the square Kt4 and then my Rook's and Knight's Pawns could continue the attack. My Pawns would control all the black squares and my Bishop the white squares to which Black's King might want to flee, so that he would have to approach my camp at my B3. Then I could drive him to my Kt2 with the Bishop and my Rooks would give him the mortal blow. As he would be advancing one rank with each move, I could foresee without any particular difficulty that he must be mate in eight moves. Thus I proceeded:

11.	Q×P ch	K×Q
12.	Kt×B dbl. ch	K—R3
13.	KKt—Kt4 ch	K—Kt4
14.	P—R4 ch	K—B5
15.	P—Kt3 ch	K—B6
16.	B—K2 ch	K—Kt7
17.	R—R2 ch	K—Kt8
18.	K—Q2 mate	

The mating position, shown in Diagram 53, is really extraordinary. The black King is completely surrounded by White's pieces in White's camp, something which to my knowledge has never happened in any other game on record. Black's faithful troops look on impotently from far away.

In connection with this game I had quite a touching

experience several years later. Shortly after coming to
this country I had occasion to visit a Chess Club in
Brooklyn as a member of the Manhattan Chess Club
team on which I played one of the boards. Before the
match started, an old man among the onlookers approached me, pulled a newspaper clipping from his
pocket which contained the record of a Chess game, and
asked me smilingly whether I knew that game. From a

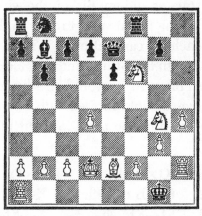

DIAGRAM 53.

glance at it I saw that it was this game I had played
against Sir George Thomas. The old man introduced
himself and said: "Let me shake hands with you. I have
seen many beautiful games in my long life, but this is
the most beautiful. I play it over whenever I feel blue,
and it makes me happy again. I always carry it in this
pocket, right over my heart."

My own pleasure at this game received quite a jolt
another few years later. One fine day I received a letter
from a Chess Club in Australia. The writer said they
had analyzed my game with Thomas and enjoyed it
very much, but he was sorry he had to disappoint me

with the information that I could have checkmated my
opponent in seven instead of eight moves, unless I had
already found this out. He appended the following variations, which I regret to say are really correct:

11.	Q×P ch	K×Q
12.	Kt×B ch	K—R3
13.	KKt—Kt4 ch	K—Kt4
14.	P—B4 ch !	

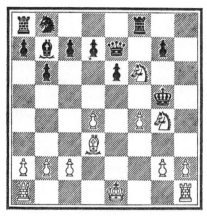

DIAGRAM 54.

This check does it the quickest way! I had not considered it in the game, because I had not seen the nice
mate in two which would follow if Black moves K×P.
15. P—Kt3, K—B6 would enable mate by 16. O—O, and
if instead the King goes back to Kt4, 16. P—R4 mates.

14.	....	K—R5
15.	P—Kt3 ch	K—R6
16.	B—B ch	B—Kt7
17.	Kt—B2 mate	

16. O—O would also have forced the mate with the

Knight. Some unaccountable aesthetic predilections most of us have seem to make the mate which actually occurred in the game appear more beautiful.

WHITE: *Edward Lasker* BLACK: *H. Holbrook*

Played in the Chicago Championship tournament 1916.

1.	P—Q4	P—Q4
2.	Kt—KB3	Kt—KB3
3.	P—B4	

The reason for this move, as explained in the discussion of the Pawn skeleton shown in Diagram 34, is to provide an open file for the Rooks to work in later on.

| 3. | .... | B—B4 |
| 4. | P—K3 | |

In order to castle as quickly as possible. Any other development move such as Kt—B3 or B—B4 would have been just as good. Worthy of consideration was also Q—Kt3, attacking the Pawn the protection of which Black's last move relinquished. Black would then have done best to defend with Q—B sq, because P—QKt3 would have weakened the square QB3 and given White the opportunity to operate in the diagonal QR4—K8 with his King's Bishop and Queen after first playing P—K3 and exchanging Pawns on Q5.

| 4. | .... | B×Kt |

Black's idea prompting this and the next move was apparently to gain the square Q4 for his Queen and incidentally to threaten my Queen's Rook's Pawn and make me lose time in defending it. But this maneuver wastes two moves to exchange a piece which has not yet moved at all and if Black had tried to evaluate his plan from the point of view of general strategic principles he would have concluded that it must be bad even though the

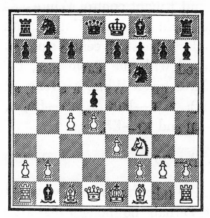

DIAGRAM 55.

reasons why are not apparent in an immediate combination. Much better would have been P—B3, opening a line for the Queen and supporting the centre Pawn. 5. Q—Kt3 could then have been answered with Q—B2 or Q—Kt3, where the Queen would have been placed actively rather than merely defending the Knight's Pawn.

5. R×B   P—B3

Threatening Q—R4 ch followed by Q×P. I decided to ignore this threat because Black would again lose two moves to capture the Pawn and meanwhile I should be able to gain a winning advantage in development. The obvious move for me to think of was 6. B—Q3, and perhaps that move was the best, since the exchange on Q5,

which I made first, takes the black Queen to a commanding centre square.

      6. P×P   Q×P

This way of recapturing is better than Kt×P because
now Queen and Knight control White's K4 while after
Kt×P White could drive the Knight with P—K4 and
gain command of almost all centre squares. Black could
have recaptured with the Pawn also, but 7. Q—Kt3
would then have given White a strong attack. For example: Q—B2; 8. B—Kt5 ch, Kt—B3; 9. B—Q2 followed by R—B and Kt—K5.

      7. B—Q3   P—K3

Black is afraid to take the Pawn in view of his backward
development. Perhaps he thought that after making this
developing move instead I would do something for my
Rook's Pawn and he would in that way catch up with another developing move. But I felt it was still worth sacrificing the Pawn against an advantage of two moves to-
ward completion of development.

      8. O—O   Q×RP
      9. B—Q2   Q—Q4

The Queen must come back into the game without delay
because I threatened to stalemate her with P—K4 and
then to catch her with B—B3 and R—R.

Quite a number of continuations look attractive for
White in this position (Diagram 56). The advance of the
King's Pawn, which would dislodge Black's Queen from
the centre, might be prepared with either Q—B2 or Q—

K2 or R—K. Of these three moves Q—B2 would probably have deserved preference because the Queen would
have been occupying an open file and prevented Black's
Knight from settling on K5.

DIAGRAM 56.

The move I actually chose, Kt—K5, must also be good
because it brings the Knight to a centre square from
which he is difficult to dislodge. He can be supported
there with P—B4 and then Black cannot very well exchange him with his Queen's Knight from Q2 because in
recapturing with the Bishop's Pawn I would be opening
a file for my King's Rook and drive away Black's King's
Knight which is sorely needed for protection of the King.

10.	Kt—K5	QKt—Q2
11.	B—B4	Q—Q3
12.	P—B4	P—KKt3

It seems that Black feared a violent attack on his King
beginning with the sacrifice 13. Kt×KBP, K×Kt; and followed up with 14. P—B5. However, if he had played
12. B—K2 which is the natural developing move sug-

gested by the position (Diagram 57) it is doubtful
whether White's attack would have succeeded, in view
of the many pieces clustered around Black's King for defense. The continuation might have been 12. ...., B—
K2; 13. Kt×KBP, K×Kt; 14. P—B5, Kt—Kt3; 15. B×P

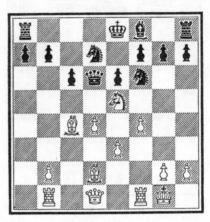

DIAGRAM 57.

ch or P×P ch, K—K; and no immediately decisive combination appears possible.

I should hardly have even thought of this sacrifice.
There were many moves at my disposal after 12. ....
B—K2 which would have well prepared the final on-
slaught, such as Q—B3, followed by P—KKt4 and P—
KKt5, or Q—B3 in conjunction with B—B3 and P—K4,
for example.

The move of the text weakens the black squares on
Black's King wing and soon gives my black Bishop an
opportunity for action.

13. R—B

I think today I would prefer Q—B3, leaving a choice of
moves open for the Queen's Rook. On B sq, however, the

Rook is unquestionably well posted. It prevents the immediate advance P—QB4 a move which Black would naturally want to make as soon as feasible, in order to obtain some pressure on White's strong centre and to open a file for his own Rook. The answer would now be 14. B—Kt5 which threatens P×P, and if Black replies P×P, 15. Q—R4 would follow, threatening B×Kt ch and B—Kt4, R—Q etc.

13.	Kt—Kt3
14. B—R2	Kt—K5
15. B—K	

Black is after my Bishops and I naturally avoid their exchange. But Black has occupied K5 and thus stemmed the advance of my King's Pawn. This shows that Q—B3 would have been better for me than R—B on the 13th move.

15.	B—K2

Black must have believed I would get a dangerous attack with P—KKt4 if he played P—KB4 instead of the

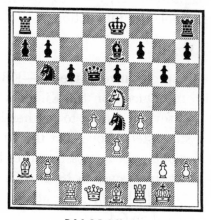

DIAGRAM 58.

Bishop move on which he decided. But P—KB4 looks like the right move in this position, since it counteracts my plan to push the King's Pawn. After 15. ....., P—KB4; 16. P—KKt4 Black might have played Kt—Q4. It was then by no means easy to find a compelling continuation. Since the centre would have been rather effectively blocked I would probably have switched the scene of action to the Queen's wing where I have open files and command more territory. 17. Q—Kt3 suggests itself, possibly with the continuation Q—B2; 18. B—Kt, KKt—B3; 19. P—Kt5, Kt—Q2; 20. P—K4 or, if 19. ....., Kt—R4, first 20. B—Q2 and then P—K4.

In view of this line of play I should probably have played P—KKt4 in the position of Diagram 58. I would then have been a move to the good as the position of Black's Bishop on K2 does not change anything as far as my threats are concerned. In fact, my attack would have been a good deal stronger, as after 16. P—KKt4, Kt—Q4 (P—KB4 is now not playable on account of P×P followed by either Kt—B7 or Q—R5 ch, depending upon how Black recaptures); 17. Q—Kt3, Q—B2; 18. P—B5 gets my King's Rook also into action.

16. Q—B3

Now I would surely have played P—KB4 in Black's place, for with my Queen on the King's wing I would have had to lose several moves to get her into position for the attack suggested above. On the King's side no forced break-through appears possible after P—KB4; 17. P—KKt4, R—KKt. In answer to 18. B—Kt, Kt—B3; 19. P—Kt5, KKt—Q2 Black will after all get his Queen's Knight solidly settled on Q4.

16. . . . .   Kt—B3

This gives me much more freedom, a choice of different attacking plans, and is therefore a positional error on
the part of my adversary, affording me a great deal of re-
lief.

17. K—R

My intention is to give up the Queen's Pawn and then
to occupy the long diagonal with my Queen's Bishop and
the Queen's file with one of my Rooks. In this plan I do
not want to be hampered by a check when the black
Queen takes my Pawn.

17. . . . .   Kt (Kt3)—Q4
18. P—K4   Kt—QKt5
19. B—Kt   Q×P

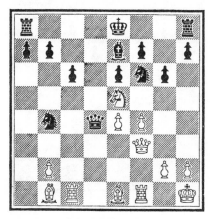

DIAGRAM 59.

He knows no fear.

20. R—B4 !

Stronger than B—B3 right away, because the Knight is
now twice attacked and needs watching. The Queen

cannot take the Knight's Pawn as B×Kt followed by
Kt—Q3 would win a piece.

| 20. . . . . | Q—Kt3 |
| 21. B—B3 | R—Q |

Evidently Black does not see my threat. Comparatively
best was probably P—B4, to get the Knight back into
play via B3. But even then Black's game was lost. I could
have either continued 22. Kt—Kt4, winning the exchange, or 22. P—B5, breaking through in the King's
Bishop's file.

22. R×Kt !	B×R
23. Kt—B4	Q—R3
24. B×Kt	O—O

DIAGRAM 60.

25. Kt—K5 !

I considered my Bishop much too beautifully placed to
give him up for a Rook who has very few squares at his
disposal. After that exchange I would have remained
with a Knight for two Pawns, but there were no more op-

portunities for a mating attack and a long drawn out
ending would have ensued. When I played Kt—K5 I
had, of course, visions of mate with the Knight on R6 or
with the Queen on Kt7, after a few preparatory maneuvers.

> 25. .... R—Q7

He did not realize that this square, which would ordinarily be ideal for the Rook, is poisoned.

> 26. B—Q3

This takes all squares away from the Rook but QKt7.

> 26. .... Q—R5
> 27. Kt—B4

And this does not even leave Kt7 open.

> 27. .... R×B

I gladly give this Bishop for the Rook, as on white
squares I cannot do much in view of the fact that most
Black Pawns are placed on White.

> 28. Q×R Q—Kt4

Black aims at the exchange of Queens, to eliminate the
danger of mating attacks.

> 29. R—B3 Q—R3

With my Rook's move I planned the combination discussed in Chapter 3, sacrificing the Rook on KR7 and
then mating with Q—R3 ch and Q—R8. Black's reply
threatens mate in case I move my Rook out of the
Bishop's file. I must therefore first guard my Queen's
Rook's square.

> 30. P—QKt3 P—QKt4

This move is, of course, not made to drive the Knight away who has several good squares at his disposal. It plans Q—Kt2 followed by B—K2, to force my Bishop out of the hole which is so dangerous for Black.

31. Kt—K3

On K5 the Knight would obstruct the diagonal of the Bishop.

31. ....   Q—Kt2
32. R—R3   B—K2

DIAGRAM 61.

33. B—Kt2

I was too keen on giving that mate in the corner! The logical continuation would no doubt have been Kt—Kt4. If then P—KR4, all sorts of brilliant mating combinations might result. For example: 34. R×P, P×R; 35. Kt—R6 ch, K—R2; 36. P—K5 ch, K×Kt; 37. Q—Kt3 and mate in three moves. Or: 34. ...., B×B; 35. Kt×B ch, K—Kt2; 36. Q—QB3, P×R; 37. Kt—K8 ch and mate on Kt7 or R8. Thus, Black would have had to take the

Bishop right away; and the consequence would have been: 34. Kt×B ch, K—Kt2; 35. Q—Q4 (threatening again mate through Kt—K8 and Q—Kt7), R—QR; 36. R×P ch, K—B; 37. Q—Q6 ch, Q—K2; 38. Kt—Q7 ch and wins the Queen.

33.	Q—B2

Had he realized my threat in all its magnitude, he would have played P—B3, in order to interrupt the diagonal of my Bishop. He intends Q—Q and B—B3.

34. R×P !!	K×R
35. Kt—Q5 !	

Threatening mate through Q—R3—R8 and at the same time attacking the Queen.

35.	Q—Q
36. Q—R3 ch	B—R5
37. B—B6 !	Resigns.

CHAPTER SEVEN

The Chess Problem

THE modern Chess Problem has no relation to a Chess game whatsoever except that the same rules govern the movement of the pieces. It is true that the Chess problem originated with the game. The early composers always concerned themselves with positions which might occur in a game and in which an unexpected move forced the win or produced a mate in a given number of moves. To-day such positions are called End-game studies, while the composer of Problems pays no attention to the question whether or not the position, or the combination made possible by it, is at all likely to occur in a game. The position of a problem is generally supposed to be one which could possibly be reached in a game, no matter how absurd from a player's point of view the moves would have to be to reach it. In my opinion this is an unnecessary restriction of problemists, because most of their positions would be absurdities in a game anyway; and while a player might find an occasion to use an idea in his combinations which he has seen in a problem, he could do so whether the exact position of the problem in question can be reached in a game or not.

This lack of relation between game and problem does not mean that the latter is not worth a player's attention. On the contrary, the problem offers a type of pleasure which, though different from the pleasure found in games, is just as intense for anyone gifted with aesthetic sensibilities.

Furthermore, it conveys to the student an insight into possibilities of combining the effect of various Chessmen which he would hardly ever obtain from playing games alone.

The Chess problem belongs decidedly in the field of artistic creation. Its construction is governed by certain aesthetic principles which, through the consensus of educated taste, have almost become law.

The leading principle is that of economy of force, and the element of surprise, which is an outstanding factor in almost anything that strikes us as beautiful, must naturally also be present in a problem to arouse our interest.

The position of Diagram 62 will illustrate the principle of economy. This problem, which is by H. Weenink, requires White to checkmate in two moves. The key move is 1. Q—B4. This threatens mate through Q×P. The theme is to force Black, no matter what defense he chooses to prevent the threatened mate, to block an existing defense against other mates. For example: If

Black plays 1. ...., B—B3, which bars the path of the Queen, he thereby blocks his Pawn and White mates with 2. Q—Kt4. If Black plays 1. ...., P—B3 instead,

DIAGRAM 62.

he blocks the line of the Bishop and White mates with 2. Q—Q4. There is a third variation which does not block a defensive piece but a flight square of the black King. If Black plays 1. ...., P—B4, White mates with 2. Q—K6.

White has only two pieces and still three neat variations are comprised in the position. Incidentally, combinations based on interference between two defending men or blocking of flight squares of the King are not infrequent in games. The position discussed in connection with Diagram 2 offered an example. That is why such a surprising first move as Nimzovich made in that position is often called a "problem move."

The sacrifice, which in a game constitutes one of the main elements of beauty, has generally no meaning in a problem, because White has usually such a vast superiority in material that giving up some of it rarely weakens his forces sufficiently to cause much surprise. Only if the piece sacrificed seems essential in one or more of the contemplated mating positions would the sacrifice be startling. The position of Diagram 63 might serve as illustration. This problem, also a two-mover, is by A. Ellerman. White must search for a first move which will cut off the escape of Black's King to his sixth rank in case he goes to B5. Then Kt—Kt6 would be mate. The first move must also cut off the King's escape into the King's Bishop's file in case Black moves K—K4. Then 2. R—KR5 would be mate. 1. Q—B would accomplish the second task and at the same time prevent the reply K—B5 altogether. If this were the solution the problem

DIAGRAM 63.

would be a very bad one. The key move should never restrict the mobility of Black's King. If anything it should increase it. Incidentally, the Knight on QB8 would be an entirely unnecessary piece in that case. We need not look very long to find the refutation of Q—B. Black would reply R—K4, providing an escape for the King on K3, and White could checkmate on the next move

only if he could reach either QR2 or QKt3 with his
Queen, which he cannot from KB sq.

The only move with the Queen which would serve all
three purposes mentioned would be 1. Q—B3. But there
she can be taken by Black's Pawn. Here is where the
surprise comes in. This Queen's sacrifice actually solves
the problem; for after P×Q White mates with 2. B—K3,
Black's escape now being cut off by White's Rook.

The aesthetic pleasure we derive from a Chess problem is unquestionably greater when there are only a few
pieces on the board and when either the mating method
or the mating position is surprising. Difficulty of solution alone, particularly when partly due to a cluttering
up of the board with many pieces, diminishes the artistic effect rather than increase it.

An outstanding example of an aesthetically moving
problem is the famous three-mover by Sam Lloyd which
is shown in Diagram 64. This is a problem which I think
could convert any Chess player into a problem fan who
had previously neglected this branch of Chess.

The first move is B—Kt3 ch. Ordinarily problems do
not start with a check because this would limit Black's
choice of moves in most cases, a method which the purist
would consider brutal. But where Black has only the
King on the board so that he would have to move him
anyway, there can of course be no objection to checking him on the first move.

Black here has the choice between K—K5, K—B3
and K—Q3. If he plays K—K5, White continues with
2. Q—B2, cutting off the King's escape to the Bishop's
file. The only move Black has then left is K—Q6, whereupon 3. Q—B3 produces a perfectly beautiful mating

DIAGRAM 64.

position. After this one would expect nothing but an anti-climax from the other variations. But Lloyd outdid himself in this composition. In answer to 1. . . . ., K—B3 White plays 2. B—Kt4, forcing K—Kt4, and now the Queen goes to QKt7, producing the same beautiful mate at right angles to the first variation.

This is not all. If the King goes to Q3 on the first move, 2. B—B4 follows. Now the King must go to B3 and 3. Q—QB7 is mate, the two Bishops, Queen and Black King again being placed in one straight line!

Composers found that to express new ideas, i.e. combinations not known from game experience, they usually needed at least three or four moves. The three-mover practically dominates the field of problem composition. One of the most fruitful ideas in three-move problem combinations was the so-called Indian idea. The line of action of a piece is first interrupted so that the black King can move into that line, and then the line is again uncovered with mate.

An elementary illustration of this type of combination

is given in Diagram 65. Black's only move is P—R5 after which he would be stalemate. White's second move must therefore be such as to make some square available for the black King. The only piece which could check-mate the King in this problem is the Bishop, and this makes the solution rather simple. The square on which White will try to mate the King is Black's KR4. But if White plays the Bishop around into the diagonal Q1—KR5, the King can return to R3 again on the third

DIAGRAM 65.

move. A checkmate is evidently possible only by a third move which not only attacks Black's KR4 but also R3. This can only be done by two white pieces at the same time, so that the final move must be a discovered check. This suggests the solution: 1. B—K8, P—R5; 2. K—B7, K—R4; 3. K—Kt7 mate.

Without being familiar with this idea it is practically impossible for a solver to find the solution of Indian problems. I remember being introduced to this form of compositions by the position of Diagram 66 when I was a boy. A problem fan offered me any bet I wanted that

I could not solve the problem in a month. I gave up after breaking my head on it for an hour. Black has again only one move, P—Kt4, after which he would be stalemate, so that White must provide a square for him on the second move. For this reason the attempt to make a Queen on the first move and to reach the Queen's Rook's file with her for a mate on the third move does not work. If, on the second move, White gives a discovered check, the King goes to R7 or the Pawn advances, and then the

DIAGRAM 66.

Bishop blocks the way of the Queen to QR8. Or, if White plays the Bishop to Kt7 or R6 on the second move, enabling the King to capture the Knight, and then returns to B8 with a check, the King has the escape to R4.

The only solution is 1. P—Kt8, promoting the Pawn into a Knight! After P—Kt4 White continues with 2. Kt—K7 !, interrupting the line of the Bishop and thus enabling K×Kt. 3. Kt—B6 then checkmates the King by opening the Bishop's file again and at the same time covering his escape to R4.

The Pawn promotion into a Knight has been frequently used by composers, so that an experienced solver would have tried the right first move before any other even if he were not acquainted with the Indian idea.

Many remarkable Indian problems have been composed with more than one variation. Often a Bishop is used to block temporarily a Rook in one variation and

DIAGRAM 67.

in another the Rook forms the temporary block of the Bishop.

Another theme frequently used is illustrated in Diagram 67, a four-mover by Von Holzhausen.

Black's King is stalemate so that any check by the Bishop or Knight would be a mate unless defended by the Rook. White cannot threaten mate with the Knight because as soon as the latter moves the Rook would check several times. He can threaten mate with the Bishop, but the Rook can always defend it. White might try to utilize a threat with the Bishop to lure the Rook to a square from which he cannot check, so that the Knight would be free to move to Q4 from where he threatens mate on Kt3 as well as on B2. B—R3, for example would force Black to play either R×B or R—QKt6. In neither case would White accomplish his purpose. After R×B, 2. Kt—Q4 the Rook would go to QB6 and both mates would be protected, and if 1. . . . ., R—QKt6 White will be interfered with again by the check on Kt8.

The solution is very pretty. White plays 1. B—Kt4, allowing the Rook to move to any square in the 6th rank. On the second move the Bishop sacrifices himself with 2. B—B3 ch. This forces the Rook to the only square from which he càn protect both mates the Knight can threaten from Q4. After 2. . . . ., R×B; 3. Kt—Q4, however, the Rook is forced to leave that square again, and on the fourth move the Knight will checkmate on whichever of these two squares the Rook leaves unprotected.

In End-game studies the composer naturally tries to preserve the semblance of a game-position. In fact, that semblance is almost an aesthetic prerequisite.

Diagram 68 shows an end-game study by Petrov which is highly amusing on account of a most astonish-

DIAGRAM 68.

ing mating combination; but, of course, the position could never be reached in an actual game, though this fact is very cleverly veiled.

White is to play and win. He starts with 1. R—K7 ch. Black cannot capture the Knight because White would play P×P and queen on the following move. Neither can he go B sq on account of R×P mate. Thus he is forced to reply 1. . . . ., K—Q3. White then continues 2. P×P. After 2. . . . ., Kt×Kt he cannot queen his Pawn because Black would reply Kt—K4 ch and capture the Queen with the Rook. But he wins by promoting the Pawn into a Knight! 3. P—B8 (Kt) ch, K—Q4; 4. Kt—Kt6 ch, K—Q3; 5. R—Q7 ch, K—K4; 6. R—Q5 ch ! The Rook

DIAGRAM 69.

must capture, and 7. Kt—B4 mate follows. The antics of White's Knight are certainly extraordinary.

Still more thinly disguised as a game-position is the following end-game by Kasparyan which also imbues a truly phantastic combination with a great deal of humor.

White, on the move, is to force a draw. He begins with 1. Kt—B4, which threatens mate through Q—Q3 or

Kt—Q5. After Q×P ch he continues with 2. Kt—Kt2 ch, forcing K—K5. Now comes a move one would not conceive of in his wildest dreams! 3. Q×R !! If Black takes the Queen, White is stalemate! Therefore, Black will try to first relieve the stalemate by giving up his own Queen also, since he would still remain with a winning superiority of material. But after 3. ...., Q—R7 ch White does not capture the Queen. He answers 4. K—B2 and again he would be stalemate if Black captured his Queen. Then Black tries 4. ...., Q—Kt8 ch. However, White escapes once more: 5. K—Kt3, and the stalemate remains unbroken, since the Knight remains pinned. After 5. ...., Q—B7; 6. K—R2 Black finds the tantalizing situation unrelieved, and all he can do is draw by perpetual check, chasing the white King in circles around the Knight.

While the last two positions are most ingeniously

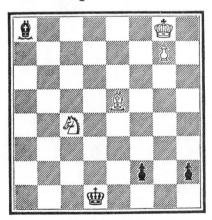

DIAGRAM 70.

composed they will really satisfy only the tyro in the art of problems and studies. Compare with them the finesse in the following two examples, which are end-

games in the true sense of the word. In both of them
White is to play and draw.

In the position of Diagram 70, a famous composition
of Henri Rinck, White can obviously stop the Rook's
Pawn only with B×P and the Bishop's Pawn only with
Kt—K3 ch. He must make the latter move first because
Black would otherwise play B—Q4 ch, capture the
Knight and queen his Bishop's Pawn. But what after 1.
Kt—K3 ch, K—K7; 2. B×P, K×Kt ? White cannot prevent Black's Pawn from queening any longer while
Black can stop White's Pawn with B—Q4. Thus Black
seems to have a sure win. But White forces the draw
by an astounding combination: 3. K—R8, B—Q4;
4. P—Kt8 (Q), B×Q; 5. B—Kt !! Now Black cannot
queen except by capturing the Bishop and White is
stalemate!

DIAGRAM 71.

Diagram 71 shows an end-game composition by
Richard Reti.

It seems well nigh impossible for White to force a
draw. He cannot catch Black's Pawn, and his own Pawn

can be stopped by the Bishop. Only if he could force
Black to lose a move could he gain the "tempo" neces-
sary to reach Black's Pawn in time. Here is the procedure
by which he accomplishes this: 1. K—K7, P—Kt4; 2.
K—Q6, P—Kt5; 3. P—K7, B—Kt4; 4. K—B5 ! This is
White's salvation. Black must move the Bishop if he is
to stop White's Pawn; but after 4. . . . ., B—K; 5. K—Q4
White's King has reached the rank on which the black
Pawn stands and ~can block his way to the queening
square. 5. . . . ., K—Kt2; 6. K—K3, K—B2; 7. K—B4,
B—R4 does not help either as 8. P—K8 (Q), B×Q; 9.
K×P leaves Black only with the Bishop.

Without knowing who composed the last two end-
game studies, the connoisseur can tell that the position
of Diagram 70 was conceived by a master-problemist and
that of Diagram 71 by a master of the game. Though
Réti's position is perhaps not very likely to occur in an
actual game, the idea behind it is "game-born," so to
speak, while Rinck's position has the ear marks of a
problemist's labor. Both have a style of their own and
thus share an attribute common to all products which can
justifiably claim to be classed as works of art.

2.

C H E S S   F O R

blood

Master Chess

N THE PRECEDING PAGES we have looked only at the pleasant side of Chess—the kind played among amateurs for the excitement of a battle without bloodshed, in which the supreme command is in their hands, but the outcome of which is of no grave consequence to either player.

There is another side to Chess, however, which is quite different—tournament and match games played by masters or those striving to become masters, whose standing, if not livelihood, may be seriously affected by the outcome.

Such games are no fun, even for the winner. They are the hardest work imaginable. You play for blood! You avoid the lure of beautiful combinations unless you see clearly that they do not endanger your chance to draw the game at least, if you cannot win it. For it is not the beauty of a combination which wins a tournament, but the number of points you make—a whole point for a win, a half a point for a draw, and an "egg" for a loss.

The professional Chess player makes preparations for his games of a type undreamed of by the amateur. He carefully studies the style of each opponent whom he has to face, by playing over as many of his games as he can find in the records of previous tournaments; to nullify similar efforts on the part of his adversary he chooses an opening quite different from those he has played in earlier rounds; he does not even necessarily play the line he considers best, but keeps that line in store for another, more dangerous opponent he may have to meet in a later round.

If your adversary is known to like a slow positional development, you try to lead the game into an opening which offers early possibilities of hand-to-hand encounters. If he likes to attack himself, you set up a granite wall of defense, in the hope of inducing him to make a premature onslaught.

If you succeed in drawing your man into a variation you have prepared for him, you do not show it by playing rapidly. On the contrary. Although you are quite certain what your next move will be, you may assume a pose of troubled thought and permit several minutes to elapse before making your move, to lull your adversary into a false feeling of security.

These are some of the pleasant little by-plays of serious, grim tournament Chess; but they become very unpleasant when you are the victim of such psychological tactics yourself!

Well, let us assume that both players have avoided

pitfalls in openings not yet fully analyzed, and a more or less even middle game has been reached. Then a silent, deadly struggle ensues for the most minute positional advantage. What wearing effort to remain constantly on your guard and to work out in your mind the positions this or that variation will lead to, though they are never reached in the actual game because your opponent chooses a different road! The emaciating concentration required to keep this network of combinations before you for fully four or even five hours at a stretch, until the game is adjourned for a dinner interval! How often fatigue dulls your wits and causes you to throw away a good game by a blunder no beginner would make! That harassing time clock! The nerve-racking excitement when you have only seconds left in which to make up your mind, where ten or fifteen minutes would not be too much! The fear that grips your throat when your opponent makes an unexpected move just as you have used up almost all the time allotted to you! The hope which quickens your pulse when he is pressed for time himself in a difficult position! Not to let him benefit by the time you are taking for your own moves, you are often tempted to play too rapidly and then one little error may throw away the fruits of hours of hard labor!

I do not think there is any other mental strain comparable to the exertion to which a tournament game subjects the Chess master. Working at what seemed to me the most difficult mathematical problems has never exhausted me nearly as much as playing in a Chess tournament; and of all intellectual applications mathematical work is surely the hardest. That is why physical fitness is a most important factor in tournament Chess and why young players, whose brains can stand the poisons of fatigue much longer than those of older players, have a great advantage.

Emanuel Lasker, who, at the age of 56 years, in the New York tournament of 1924, was able to go through twenty rounds and win the contest against the strongest players of that day, and who, even at the age of 67, came very near to duplicating that feat in Moscow, has established a most astounding record—an exception which does not disprove the rule. No other player has ever remotely approached this achievement.

I recall an interesting conversation I had with him a few days before the memorable New York tournament —the only serious contest in which I had occasion to cross swords with him. While taking a walk in Central Park we were discussing the chances of the various participants. I had not seen any of the European masters since the outbreak of the World War and I did not know what to expect of them, though here and there I had played over a game from the records of European tournaments held during the preceding five years.

Emanuel Lasker said to me: "I am sorry to discourage you; but no matter how well you play today—I haven't seen you in many years—I am afraid you have no chance against these young players. They have done nothing during the last five years but analyze and practice every conceivable variation of the modern openings and they know the best moves in all of them. You will have to spend a great deal of time in every game trying to find your way through these new openings. Let us say it takes you only twenty or thirty minutes to do so, and let us even assume you find the best line of play. They will have consumed no more than five minutes for the same number of moves—and how can anybody give a first class master the odds of twenty five or even fifteen minutes? I don't think I have much of a chance against these young fellows myself."

I ventured to suggest that one might try to force the game into one of the classical channels. But he shook his head and said: "You will see that Chess has become much more difficult since the advent of modernism."

In the light of this conversation Emanuel Lasker's victory—1½ points ahead of Capablanca, then the World champion—was indeed a brilliant achievement. As Horace Bigelow, who covered the tournament for one of the New York papers, remarked at the time: "The modern school came, saw and succumbed."

To afford the reader an inkling of what one has to go through in a tournament game I am giving a move by move explanation of two games I played myself against some of the leading masters. By reviewing only games of my own I can supply not only a fairly accurate analysis but also a description of the psychological background which, as I said before, is often quite as important for their full understanding.

Another reason why I have confined myself to games I have played myself is that it is extremely difficult to analyze someone else's games correctly. Even so brilliant a Chess writer and analyst as the present World champion, Alexandre Alekhine, has made a good many errors in the analyses of games played by others which he supplied for the printed records of various tournaments.

An example is the game I played against Emanuel Lasker in the New York tournament. Alekhine overlooked the crucial move in one of the variations of a combination which I had at my disposal on the thirtieth turn. Thus he arrived at the conclusion that my position was lost or at least unfavorable, and he misjudged the whole development leading up to it, while in fact my game was won just at that point.

Such errors are only too human, particularly when an editor must analyze a whole series of games within a rather limited time. They do not detract from the great value these tournament records have for the student, as the most important thing in them is always the explanation of the larger strategic plans which form the basis of a master game, and not the analysis of specific tactical maneuvers. In the unfolding of the strategic background of the different openings Alekhine is a past master, and the glossaries in his books in which he discusses his games are the best post-graduate course I could think of for any student.

The frame of mind in which I gave my great namesake battle was none too auspicious. It was the sixth round of the tournament, and I had made only 1½ points in the first five rounds, having drawn the first three games and lost the following two. In the first game, against Maroczy, and in the second, against Bogoljuboff, I had been outplayed in the opening and had drifted into cramped positions from which there seemed no hope of escape. In both games I did escape through a temporary Pawn sacrifice which my esteemed opponents took insufficient trouble in analyzing to the end. Most likely they underestimated me a little, since I was the only amateur who had been admitted into this most illustrious gathering of professional Chess masters ever

assembled. Had not one of the speakers at the banquet
preceding the tournament referred to me teasingly as
"Lasker common" and to my name-sake as "Lasker preferred"? I had hardly expected to benefit from the psychological effect of this situation to the extent of two
half points. In fact, I almost won the game against
Bogoljuboff. The effect of my Pawn sacrifice had de-
moralized him a bit, and I was able to sacrifice a Rook
soon afterward which he should not have accepted. But
in the excitement of time trouble I missed the winning
move.

My opponent in the third round was Capablanca, and
to make things worse I had the black pieces. I had
played a good deal with him and, like many others, had
emerged with the disagreeable feeling that he was un-
beatable. This feeling, naturally, did not help my spirits
on this new occasion. The world champion seemed indeed to have me in difficulties in the early middle-game,
but somehow I worked out of them into an even position
and gladly accepted the draw he offered.

If this result—1½ out of three tough points—made
me sufficiently cocky to say to Emanuel Lasker: "Well,
your moderns seem to be better in position play than in
combinations!", I was shaken all the worse by the outcome of my fourth and fifth games.

In the fourth round I faced Yates and after about
twenty moves had him in such trouble that mentally I
scored my first victory on the board. However, he extri-
cated himself with an ingenious maneuver, and playing
indifferently from then on I lost not only my positional
advantage but the game.

In the fifth round I played Janowski and maintained

the upper hand from the opening through the middle-game. At one point I had three different continuations at my disposal each of which would have forced the win very quickly. But I made two blunders in succession and lost—as Alekhine said in his analysis of that game in the tournament book: "Two miracles had to happen to save Janowski, and they did happen."

Thus, when I met Emanuel Lasker in the sixth round, I was certainly anything but hopeful of my chances. But I was thrilled by the thought of a serious game with the greatest Chess master of all times whose name was accidentally also my own; and I was determined to do that name honor no matter what the outcome of the battle might be.

Emanuel Lasker WHITE

vs.

Edward Lasker BLACK

AFTER considering a few minutes what opening to choose Emanuel Lasker started the game with his favorite move, P—K4. I knew I would face a Ruy Lopez if I also played P—K4, and a Ruy Lopez of a very mature variety at that, one which had the background of thirty years of World championship battles. But there was not much I could do about it. The French or the Sicilian defence, or the Caro-Kann were surely terra cognita for my opponent just as much as for me. If I went into a Ruy Lopez I had at least the advantage of familiarity with a rather recent analysis of an attack Marshall had invented. I had shown it to Emanuel Lasker cursorily a few days previously, but he had hardly had an opportunity to analyze this line carefully. In case I could not get up the courage to try the Marshall attack . . . after all a somewhat dubious innovation . . . I thought I might try a new variation of the Tarrasch defence which I had discussed with Maroczy shortly before the tournament. Very well then:

1.	P—K4	P—K4
2.	Kt—KB3	Kt—QB3
3.	B—Kt5	P—QR3
4.	B—R4	

White had hesitated a little before making this customary move, and for a moment I thought the possibility of my playing the Marshall attack might induce him to play instead one of his old favorite variations, the exchange on B6 followed by P—Q4, with the idea of producing an early favorable end-game through the Pawn majority on the King's side. True enough, Tarrasch had said: "Before the end-game the Gods have placed the middle-game," but he had lost this variation against Lasker in the first game of their World championship match all the same. Also, I had reminiscent visons of the beautiful game Emanuel Lasker had won with this opening against Capablanca at St. Petersburg in 1914, and I was just trying to remember what line of play had been analyzed to give the best defence, when White's reply relieved me of further worry in this connection.

4.	. . . .	Kt—B3
5.	O—O	B—K2

For a furtive moment I considered Kt×P instead which—as I remembered vaguely—Schlechter had played quite successfully against Lasker in 1910, in the only World championship match that had ended in a draw. However, I did not know that variation very thoroughly and preferred to steer clear of unknown complications.

| 6. R—K1 | P—QKt4 |
| 7. B—Kt3 | O—O |

Castling instead of the customary P—Q3 enables the Marshall attack in case White plays 8. P—B3. Black sacrifices a Pawn with P—Q4, 9. P×P, Kt×P; 10. Kt×P, Kt×Kt; 11. R×Kt, P—B3, or even two Pawns with 9. . . . ., P—K5; 10. P×Kt, P×Kt; 11. Q×P, B—KKt5;

DIAGRAM 72.

12. Q—Kt3, R—K. In the first alternative the continuation 11. . . . ., Kt—B3; 12. R—K, B—Q3; 13. P—Q4, Kt—Kt5 is no longer played since Marshall lost the famous game against Capablanca in which he tried this attack for the first time after an exhaustive secret analysis.

When I played O—O I was really only bluffing and

I had made up my mind by this time to play the Tarrasch defence should my illustrious opponent call my
bluff with 8. P—B3. But I thought he might perhaps
fear the complications of this attack which were by no
means easy to unravel in a time-limit game. He took
indeed quite some time before deciding upon his course.
Finally, however, shrugging his shoulders, he answered

> 8. P—B3

and the Tarrasch defence was forming, after I had sup-
pressed the last lingering desire to venture into P—Q4.

> 8. ....   P—Q3
> 9. P—KR3

A very important move in this variation, in order to
avoid the pin B—Kt5 which would greatly weaken the
effectiveness of the planned advance of the Queen's
Pawn.

> 9. ....   Kt—QR4
> 10. B—B2   P—B4
> 11. P—Q4   Q—B2

Up to this point the game has followed what is probably the most frequently played variation of the Ruy
Lopez.

> 12. QKt—Q2   BP×P

Tarrasch played Kt—B3 in this position. White then
has the choice between offering—temporarily—a Pawn
with 13. Kt—B or playing P—Q5, thus bottling up the
centre and getting set for a King's side attack. The plan
initiated with BP×P in conjunction with my next move

is an early occupation of the Queen's Bishop's file with one of the Rooks, taking advantage of the retarded development of White's Queen's wing.

I hoped this new line might make matters a little more

DIAGRAM 73.

difficult for my adversary than any other defence I might have chosen.

13. P×P	B—Q2
14. Kt—B	KR—B

Although it does not look unreasonable to use the King's Rook in this file and to keep the Queen's Rook in readiness for operations in the Queen's Rook's or Knight's file, I soon came to realize that the King's Rook would have been more useful on the King's side.

15. R—K2

This move surprised me. I had expected B—Q3, and from the result of another game played with this opening in the same tournament later that move is probably better. It may be that on K2 White thought the Rook

would serve two purposes: To protect the second rank
and to be in readiness for doubling Rooks in any file in
which they may later be required to act.

In trying to find a way to take advantage of the somewhat unnatural position of this white Rook the move
Kt—KR4 occurred to me. The Knight would threaten
to attack the Rook on B5, and if White exchanged his

DIAGRAM 74.

Bishop for the Knight my Pawn on B5 would control K6
and Kt6, the two squares which White's Queen's Knight
intended to have at his disposal.

While studying the possible consequences of this
move I saw that it involved the sacrifice of a Pawn, as
White could take twice on his K5; then, if I captured
his Knight with my Queen, he would take my Bishop
with his.

But could I not give up my Bishop on KR6 and get a
Pawn for it before taking the Knight on K5 ? Then he
would in turn first take my King's Bishop's Pawn with
his Knight. Heavens! I could not take that Knight! He
would check me with his Queen on Q5, and after I in-

terposed my Bishop he would take my Knight with check and have a winning attack.

No, there must be something else. Let us see again: I would play Kt—KR4 and then would follow: 16. P×P, P×P; 17. Kt×P, B×P; 18. Kt×P. Why could I not go back to K3 with the Bishop, attacking the Knight and defending the check threatened on my Q4? Then he must play Kt—Kt5, and I can answer Kt—B5 (Diagram 75). His Rook can't go to Q2 or K3 where he would block the Bishop who defends his Knight. He could play R—K1, discovering an attack on my Knight by his Queen, but then Kt—B5 would assure me of a strong initiative well worth the Pawn sacrificed. He would have to exchange his Queen's Bishop for my Knight, conceding to me the advantage of two mobile Bishops and attacking chances in the open Queen's file for my Rooks, for if he withdrew his threatened Knight to B3, I could badly cramp his game by R—Q1 followed by Kt—K7 ch and Q—B4. And so I jumped:

15.	Kt—R4
16. P×P	P×P
17. Kt×P	B×P
18. Kt×P	B—K3
19. Kt—Kt5	B—B5

I did not consider any other move here because I thought I was obtaining a clear advantage. Had I seen the ingenious reply my great opponent had prepared I should have considered the alternative continuation B×Kt, 20. B×B, Q—K4; this would have brought the Queen over to the King's wing with tempo and White's game would have been difficult. For example: 21. B—Q2, Kt—QB5; 22. B—B3, Q—Kt4, threatening Kt—B5.

DIAGRAM 75.

20. B—Q3   R—Q
21. R—B2 !

This almost humorous counter-pin I had not taken
into consideration. It enables White to "get out from
under." What I had been looking into while White
pondered his last move was 21. B×B, Q×B; 22. Q—B2,
Q×Q; 23. R×Q, R—Q8; 24. Kt—B3, Kt—KB5 and I
could not see a satisfactory continuation for White. 25.
R—Q2 I could have answered with R—Q, and White
would not have time to save himself with P—QKt3,
because after the exchange of Rooks Kt—Q6 would
win the Bishop or at least the exchange. 25. P—QKt3
would not defend the threat Kt—Q6 either. Again, if
25. P—KKt3, Kt—Q6; 26. K—Kt2, in order to play
Kt—K3, Black would win with R—KB! 27. Kt—K3?,
R×Kt followed by Kt—K8 ch etc. or 27. Kt (B sq)—Q2,
B—Kt4 !!; 28. Kt×B ?, R×P ch and mate in two.

With the text move White avoids all these troubles,
but I still have quite an advantage in mobility and I
control the Queen's file, so that my positional superiority

should be worth the Pawn I lost in the mix-up. Encouraging myself with these considerations I continued:

21.	....	Kt—B5
22.	B×Kt	Q×B
23.	Kt—R3	Q—K4

White will have a hard time driving me from this dominating square.

24.	B×B ch	Kt×B
25.	Q—K2	R—Q5
26.	P—B3	

The black squares around White's King are now so loosened up that my Bishop should find a fertile field of activity. First, of course, I must double Rooks in the Queen's file to prevent White from opposing his Queen's Rook.

26.	....	QR—Q
27.	QR—B	

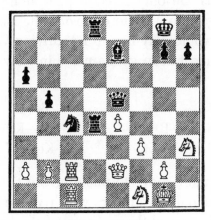

DIAGRAM 76.

Now White is ready to drive my Knight with P—QKt3 and then to operate in the open file, threatening, among other things, to exchange Rooks with R—B8. In looking around for a good spot for the Knight my conclusion was that only Q7 was really desirable. After Kt—Q3 White would be able to drive my Queen with R—B5. Kt—Kt3 did not look good either on account of 28. R—B6, QR—Q3; 29. R—B5. If I could plant the Knight on Q7, from where I threatened to exchange the Knight on White's KB sq, I would deprive the black squares around White's King of the protection the Knight now affords them, and my Bishop would thus find a welcome increase in the range of his influence.

To enable Kt—Q7 I would have to play my Bishop to Kt5 first, and I would have to be careful not to have my Knight trapped after White evaded the exchange, through Kt—R2, let us say, and attacked it for the third time with R—Q.

I had only about five minutes left within which to complete my thirtieth move, and realizing that breaking in at Q7 was the only forceful plan at my disposal I decided to go into it. Before moving the Bishop to Kt5 I thought I would play him to B4, driving White's King into the corner, just to gain a move in view of the time pressure.

27.	....	B—B4
28.	K—R	B—Kt5
29.	P—QKt3	Kt—Q7

Only one more move to make before time control. I went over the only two moves which White could make if he wanted to avoid the exchange of the Knight, either

Kt—R2 or Kt—K3. In the latter case, why could I not sacrifice my Knight on K5 and regain the piece after P×Kt, R×P, since his Knight was pinned? Well, I did not suppose White would make that move. But I awoke from my musings with a start:

30. Kt—K3 !?

He did make that move! Had he made it to complicate things so that I would not have enough time left to calculate the consequences of the sacrifice Kt×P ? Or had I made a mistake in my calculation? In feverish haste I went over the combination again. What could he do after 31. P×Kt, R×P ? Perhaps 32. R—B8 ? Then I could not

DIAGRAM 77.

exchange Rooks because after 33. R×R ch and 34. Q—B3 ch I had no defence. But what about 32. ....., R—K ? Would that not defend the first rank and still win back the Knight? After exchanging Rooks White could not protect the Knight with the other Rook because my Bishop held both White's K sq and QB3. Or could he perhaps play for a mating attack with 34.

Q—Q3 ? Tick, tick went the clock .... fifteen seconds left .... after R×Kt he would continue with 35. Q—Q5 ch. Why not interpose the Queen on K3 or even go in the corner with the King? Or could he play 34. Kt—Kt sq and answer R×Kt with Q—Kt4, attacking my Bishop and threatening R—B8 ? B—B sq should do in that case .... Three seconds left! I had to move. I was so excited by that time that the pieces began to dance in front of my eyes! Was there perhaps a move which maintained my threat .... which did not spoil anything, so that I could squeeze in my thirtieth move before the flag fell and then analyze the consequences of the Knight's sacrifice in peace? .... Ah! .... B—R6 ! His Rook must move and .... quick!

30.   ....   B—R6

I made the move just in time to avoid forfeiting the game, but immediately realized I had thrown away my opportunity to win, for after

31. R—Q

my Rook on Q sq would be en prise if, after sacrificing my Knight on K5, I played R×P.

I was worn out by the harassing time pressure and disconsolate when finding out, upon figuring through the combination again slowly, that in answer to 32. R—B8 I would really have won through R—K. A careful analysis of the combination with Emanuel Lasker himself in 1940 brought out that if he had played R—B8 on the thirtieth move, instead of Kt—K3, the game would have ended in a draw, and so I feel somewhat consoled today. After 30. ....., Kt×Kt; 31. R×R ch, R×R; 32. Q×Kt,

B—Q3; 33. P—B4, Q×KP would have been the likely
continuation. White could hardly have tried to hold the
Pawn by 33. Q—KKt, because Q—Kt6 would have
tied up his Queen and Knight. For example: 34. R—Q,
R—QB; 35. R—Q5, P—R3; Now Black threatens R—B6
and R×BP after first withdrawing his Bishop so that
White cannot play R×B in answer to R×P.

Should White forestall this threat with 36. R—Q3,
Black would continue with R—B4, threatening R—R4
and R×Kt. 37. R—K3 does not parry this threat because
Black would prevent P—B4 with B—B5, forcing 38.
Kt×B, Q×Kt. It is very doubtful whether White can
escape with a draw in this position. 39. P—KKt4 would
be frustrated through P—KR4 and 39. Q—K would be
met with R—B7, threatening not only R×P but mainly
Q—Kt4.

Alekhine, in his comments on the game, considered
my move with the Knight to Q7 an act of desperation
and put an exclamation mark after White's Kt—K3, not
realizing that my Knight's move and the sacrifice intended with it were correct and that White's answer
should have lost the game. He overlooked my move 32.
. . . ., R—K in reply to R—B8. It is a pity that through
this error he had a wrong slant on the whole strategy of
this interesting and exciting new defence which turned
into a wild attack. It would have been worth while for
the readers of his tournament book to see his notes on
the game from an angle undistorted by his oversight.

I had to seal my next move, the game being adjourned
until the evening session. Having completed the first
thirty moves within the two hours allotted for them I
had plenty of time to survey the situation.

As I could not protect my Knight with Q—Q3 on account of 32. Kt—B5, I had only B—Kt5 and the sacrifice Kt×KP, which offered considerable attacking chances even though I could no longer regain the Knight. After 32. P×Kt I could play B—Q3. If then 33. Kt—B, R×P; 34. Q—Q3 ? B—B2; 35. Q—KB3, R×R; 36. Q×R, R—K8 winning the Queen on account of the threat Q—R7 mate. I realized very soon, of course, that I was merely dreaming. For instead of Kt—B he could play much stronger 33. Kt—Kt4, R×R ch; 34. Q×R, Q—Kt6; 35. P—K5. I could not see any really promising continuation after that.

In connection with my other alternative, however, 31. ...., B—Kt5, a beautiful sacrificing combination occurred to me. It was evident that White would chase this Bishop in order to win my Knight. After 32. P—R3, B—R4; 33. P—Kt4, B—B2 I would be threatening mate, but after 34. P—B4 the mate was defended and my Queen was attacked and the Knight could not be defended with Q—Q3 on account of 35. Kt—B5. Therefore my game seemed lost . . . at least I hoped my opponent would think so. But here Kt×P loomed as the saving move which might even turn the game again in my favor! It took me fully fifteen minutes to figure through the maze of combinations connected with this variation, so that I had only 45 minutes left for the next 14 moves after which the time would be checked again. I had to make up my mind and I sealed

31. ....   B—Kt5

When the game was resumed two hours later Emanuel Lasker made the next three moves which I had expected:

       32. P—R3   B—R4
       33. P—QKt4   B—B2
       34. P—B4

and the critical position of Diagram 78 was reached.

DIAGRAM 78.

White could not have defended the mate with 34.
Kt—Kt4, because Kt×KP would have won a piece: 35.
R×R, Kt—Kt6 ch; 36. K—R2, Kt×Q ch; 37. Kt×Q,
B×Kt ch etc. He made the move P—B4 much too fast
to suit me, because it was evident that in the dinner interval he had thoroughly analyzed the combination.
Therefore I looked again carefully whether there was
anything wrong with my intended Kt×KP. After 35.
P×Q, Kt—Kt6 ch; 36. K—R2, Kt×Q he could not play
37. R×R on account of B×P ch and Kt×R. He would
have to play 37. R×B, R×R; 38. Kt×R, R×Kt; Then 39.
Kt—Kt5 was not agreeable for me, I noticed, though
R—Q; 40. R—R7, P—R3; 41. Kt—K6, R—K would
very likely have drawn. I was disappointed to realize
that this was all there was to hope for me even after my

surprise-move. But there was nothing else to be done
and so I played:

34. . . . .   Kt×KP !

My opponent again did not think very long . . . . most
disconcerting . . . . before he made a reply I had not considered at all and which proved to refute my beautiful
combination.

35. K—R2 !!

There I was! The check-Queen on Kt6 was now defended and my Queen remained attacked and had no
move to keep the Bishop guarded. In answer to Q—Q3
White would simply first exchange Rooks and then win
the Bishop; and Q—K2 was not feasible on account of
Kt—B5. In this desperate situation I had what I thought
was a brilliant stroke which saved my game. But the idea
was too beautiful to be true;

35. . . . .   R×R !!

If now 36. P×Q, then B×P ch; 37. P—Kt3, R—Q7,
winning back the Queen. Or if 36. Kt—B4, B×Kt ch; 37.
K—R3, R—Q6 etc. But the simple recapture

36. Kt×R

refutes my combination. Now my Queen must move, and
either the Bishop or the Knight is lost.

36. . . . .   Q—K2
37. R×B ?

An error of a type the old Russian Champion Ossip
Bernstein used to describe as the "equalizing injustice

of Chess." Emanuel Lasker made the move without a moment's hesitation. Evidently he had planned it far ahead, at the time he played K—R2, and as he saw he won the exchange, he did not bother looking around for other possibilities. With Kt(Q1)—B2 he would have won a whole piece and the game. R—Q5 would not have helped me because of 38. Q—K3, B—Kt3; 39. R—B8 ch, K—B2; 40. Kt×Kt, R×Kt; 41. Q×R followed by Kt—Kt5 ch.

After winning Knight and Bishop for his Rook, White has by no means an easy ending. In fact, it is doubtful whether this ending can be won at all. In view of the weak QR Pawn White must even be careful not to exchange Queens because the Rook can shift his attacks quickly from one wing to the other while the Knights cannot follow as rapidly.

Emanuel Lasker avoids the exchange of Queens and manages to work up an attack on the King in a masterly fashion

| 37. . . . . | Q×R |
| 38. Q×Kt | Q—B5 |

Of course not R×Kt on account of K—Q8 mate.

| 39. Q—K7 | Q—B |

I am trying to prevent the Knights from approaching. Kt—K3 cannot be played now because R—K would follow.

| 40. Kt(Q1)—B2 | |

With Kt—Kt5, R×Kt; 41. Q—B7 ch, K—R; 42. Q—R5, P—R3; 43. Q×R, P×Kt; 44. Q—R5 ch and

Q×P White could have produced an ending with four against three Pawns, but it is highly problematic whether it could have been won.

> 40. ....   P—R3
> 41. Q—R7

KT—K4 would have been rather disagreeable for me, because White could then have answered R—K with 42.

DIAGRAM 79.

Q—B5. The exchange of Queens would not have been favorable for me in that position as White would have captured my QR Pawn while I won his, and then he could have defended his Kt Pawn by Kt—Q3, so that I could not have obtained a passed Pawn.

> 41. ....   Q—K3

Now I keep the Kt from K4 for quite a while.

> 42. Q—Kt7   Q—Q4
> 43. Q—Kt6

If Q×RP instead, I win back the Pawn with R—QR and then the White QKt Pawn would soon also fall.

43.	R—Q3
44. Q—K3	R—K3
45. Q—QB3	Q—B5
46. Q—KB3	Q—B3
47. Q—Q3	R—Q3
48. Q—Kt3 ch	Q—Q4
49. Q—Kt	R—K3

Again Kt—K4 is prevented and now I threaten to attack the QR Pawn with R—K6. 50. Kt—Q3 is not a satisfactory defense because

DIAGRAM 80.

after R—K7; 51. Kt(R3)—B2, R—R7; 52. Q—QB, Q—B5 the Pawn falls after all. White therefore decides to take a chance and sacrifice his Knight on R6 in order to lay bare my King and to attack him with the Queen, the remaining Knight and the two connected passed Pawns.

| 50. Kt—Kt4 | R—K7 |

In permitting the sacrifice I practically offered a draw, because White's Queen will hardly have any difficulties

in enforcing a perpetual check. However, from a psychological standpoint, I felt I had winning chances because
White would try for a win with the Knight and two
passed Pawns against my Rook. I did not think I had
much to fear from such an attempt, as the White King
was bound to become exposed to attack as soon as the
Pawns advanced. I might otherwise have tried R—K5
and played R—K7 only after White's Kt—K5.

51.	Kt×P ch	P×Kt
52.	Q—Kt6 ch	K—B
53.	Q×P ch	K—K
54.	Q—Kt6 ch	K—Q

White could now draw with perpetual check, beginning with 55. Q—Kt6 and then checking on the eighth

DIAGRAM 81.

and seventh rows until I interpose either Rook or Queen,
thus relinquishing the mating threat on White's KKt2. If
White then again attacks my Rook's Pawn I have nothing
better than to repeat the threat to mate on KKt7. However, White decides to play on for a while, probably

thinking that his chance to draw by perpetual check
would remain available to him, while he might obtain
winning chances in case I took my Rook or Queen out of
play by capturing his QR Pawn.

55. Q—Kt3

Now I saw a chance to avoid perpetual check while
maintaining the mating threat with my Rook in the KKt
file.

55.		R—K
56.	Q—B2	R—Kt
57.	Q—Kt2	Q—Q3

This guards the King against checks and at the same
time keeps the Knight from approaching as long as the
Bishop's Pawn is not protected. White now maneuvers
his Queen with great finesse so as to finally secure the
cooperation of the Knight on Kt5. But meanwhile I capture White's Rook's Pawn without giving another opportunity for perpetual check, and thus obtain a winning
position.

58.	Q—B3	K—Q2
59.	Q—KB3	K—B2
60.	Q—K4	R—Kt2
61.	Q—B5	R—K2

I cannot prevent the Knight from occupying Kt5 any
longer and therefore go ahead after the Rook's Pawn.
White here sealed his move. A third four-hour session
was in prospect as the ending was evidently going to be
extremely difficult for both sides.

| 62. Kt—Kt5 | R—K6 |
| 63. Kt—K4 | Q—K2 ! |

Threatening mate in two moves.

| 64. Kt—B6 | K—Kt ! |

DIAGRAM 82.

| 65. P—Kt3 | R×RP |
| 66. K—R3 | R—R8 |

Of course not Q×P as this would allow perpetual check through 67. Q—K5, K—Kt2; 68. Q—Q5, etc.

| 67. Kt—Q5 | R—R8 ch |

For a while I considered Q—R2 ch; 68. Q×Q, R—R8 ch etc. But White could have answered 68. K—Kt4 and this would have advanced his King dangerously. In reply to the Rook check, White must retreat with the King because K—Kt4 would be followed by Q—K7 ch, etc.

| 68. K—Kt2 | Q—KR2 |

White is now forced to exchange as he has only one check and his King would not be able to stand the combined attack of Rook and Queen.

69. Q×Q	R×Q
70. K—B3	K—Kt2
71. P—Kt4	K—B3
72. K—K4	R—R

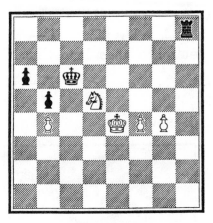

DIAGRAM 83.

My plan is, of course, to drive the Knight first and then to advance the Rook's Pawn to clear the way for the Knight's Pawn. I am threatening check on K sq, winning the Knight, so that the latter must now move. I could have accomplished the same thing by attacking the Knight directly with R—Q2, but I thought the two moves resulted in exactly the same play. I could not possibly foresee that with my Rook on the eighth instead of the seventh rank, White would have a hidden possibility of drawing. In answer to R—Q2, White could have saved his game neither with 73. Kt—B6, R—Q; 74. P—Kt5, P—R4; 75. P×P, P—Kt5 etc.; nor with 73. P—Kt5, R×Kt; 74. P—Kt6, R—Q8 etc.; nor with 73. Kt—K3, P—R4; 74. P×P, P—Kt5; 75. P—Kt5, K—B4 !; 76. Kt—B2, P—Kt6; 77. Kt—R3, K—Kt5; 78. Kt—Kt, R—Q8 etc.

73. Kt—K3	R—K ch
74. K—Q4	R—Q ch
75. K—K4	

K—B3 would have been less promising. I intended to play P—R4; 76. P×P, K—B4 ! 77. P—Kt5, P—Kt5 ch; and if 78. K—B2, P—Kt6 ch; 79. K—Kt2, R—Q7 ch; though it is doubtful whether I actually had a forced win

75.	P—R4
76. P×P	P—Kt5
77. P—R6 !	

DIAGRAM 84.

P—Kt5 would lose: P—Kt6; 78. Kt—B4, K—B4; 79. Kt—Kt2, R—Q7; 80. Kt—Q3 ch, K—B5; 81. Kt—K5 ch, K—B6 etc.

| 77. . . . . | K—B4 |

Had I realized that White had a chance to draw, as alluded to in the annotation of the 72nd move, I should have looked very much more thoroughly into the variations resulting from P—Kt6. I only figured ahead as far as 78. Kt–B4, K–Kt4; 79. Kt–Kt2, K×P; 80. K–K3 (to prevent R–Q7), K–Kt4; 81. P–Kt5; K–Kt5; 82. P–Kt6, K–B6; 83. Kt–R4, K–B7 (Diagram 84A); 84. P–B5. At this point I abandoned further analysis, as the alternative 77. . . . , K–B4, which kept my King closer to White's dangerous passed Pawns, seemed wiser.

Alekhine, in his notes to this game, did not even consider the variation sketched above feasible. Naturally I analyzed it again when going over the game for inclusion in this book, and I concluded that the position of Diagram 84A is actually won for Black if he attacks the Knight, which keeps his Pawn from advancing, with R–QR after first getting White's King into the fourth rank, so that the Knight is captured with check. This made me claim that 84. P–B5, R–K ch; 85. K–B3, R–KB would seal White's fate. If after 86. K–B4, R–QR White plays Kt–Kt6, he does not get a Queen at all. But two readers pointed out correctly that White need not play 86. K–B4. He can draw with P–Kt7, R×P ch; 87. K–Kt4, R–B8; 89. K–Kt5, winning the Rook in the end.

DIAGRAM 84A

78. P–R7 !!

Here is the surprise, which demonstrates how important a difference the position of my Rook on the eighth
row constitutes. If the Rook had gone to Q2 on the 72nd
move, he could now simply capture the Pawn. As it is, he
must lose a move for this purpose, and that is enough to
secure a draw!

78.	P—Kt6
79. Kt—Q !	R—QR

The only chance to win. K—Kt3 would be answered
with 80. K—K3, K×P; 81. Kt—Kt2, K—Kt3; 82. P—B5,
K—B4; 83. P—B6 and a similar ending to the actual
continuation.

80. P—Kt5	R×P
81. P—Kt6	R—Q2
82. Kt—Kt2	R—Q7

DIAGRAM 85.

83. K—B3 !	R—Q

Obviously, I cannot take the Knight as White's Knight's
Pawn would queen. But I can win both Pawns, and I
thought I still saw a possibility of winning the game.

84. K—K4   R—Q7

This repetition of moves is merely a maneuver to gain time for the ensuing difficult ending.

85. K—B3	R—Q
86. K—K4	K—Q3
87. K—Q4	R—QB
88. P—Kt7 !	

In order to force the Rook to get off the Bishop file so that the White King can approach my Pawn.

88.	K—K3
89. P—Kt8 (Q)	R×Q
90. K—B4	R—Kt6 !

This is the move I had calculated would win my game after all. The other contestants also believed I had now a fairly easy win as White could not capture my Pawn. I remember I left the room at this stage to stretch a little and was congratulated upon my victory by Bogoljuboff and others who were in the Press room and told me the story of the game was ready to be released. However, when I returned to the table, a rude shock awaited me.

91. Kt—R4	K—B4
92. K—Kt4	K×P

It would take White three more moves, I had calculated, to capture the Pawn: K—R3, Kt—B5 and Kt×P. But at that moment my King would reach the square QB5 and the Knight would be lost because the Rook pins it! It never occurred to me that White need not capture the Pawn at all and could still draw the game. Emanuel

Lasker actually discovered a new end-game position in which a Rook and a Pawn cannot win against the Knight, and this position has since become a classic. By a strange coincidence, the same ending occurred two or three years later in a tournament in Chicago in a game between two

DIAGRAM 86.

players one of whom happened to know this ending between Emanuel Lasker and myself and who saved a lost position because the other did not know Emanuel Lasker's discovery.

93. Kt—Kt2 !

I was certainly surprised when I saw this move. Examining the position carefully, I soon realized that I had no way of driving White's King away. And I could not cross the sixth rank without exposing the Pawn to capture! The first thing I did was to rush back to the Press room and tell the reporters that they should kill their story. I was afraid they might have already released it, for everyone had been telling them I had an easy win. Then I returned for another analysis of the position. If I could reach Q7 with the King by playing him in back of my Rook, I could still win. And I made a last attempt:

93.	....	K—K5
94.	Kt—R4	K—Q5
95.	Kt—Kt2	R—KB6
96.	Kt—R4	R—K6
97.	Kt—Kt2	K—K5
98.	Kt—R4	K—B6
99.	K—R3	

This foils my plan. After K—K7 White would play K—Kt2 and I could never approach.

99.	....	K—K5
100.	K—Kt4	K—Q5
101.	Kt—Kt2	R—R6
102.	Kt—R4	K—Q6
103.	K×P	K—Q5 ch

and we called the game a draw. It was generally considered the most exciting game of the tournament.

I felt quite discouraged, naturally, at seeing the win slip through my hands after more than thirteen hours of hard struggle. But when the excitement had subsided I came to regard this game as one of my best efforts; and whenever I think of it I smile, remembering the "equalizing injustice of Chess."

Tournament Ethics

T ONE TIME OR another almost every tournament player faces the moral problem whether or not to do his best in a game the outcome of which does not affect his own standing in the tournament. As far as I am concerned, and, I am sure, in the eyes of any impartial judge, such a problem does not really exist. If the outcome affects the relative standing of another competitor—as it almost always does —it seems to me obviously unethical for a player not to try his best. All the same, when a player is so far ahead of the rest of the field that in the last round or two he can be satisfied with a draw, he rarely puts up a real fight but merely tries to get through the game as quickly as possible without losing. That is why in some tournaments a rule has been introduced that it is not permitted to call a game a draw before at least thirty moves have been made. Unfortunately, such rules can, of course, be circumvented by a repetition of moves on which the two players agree. I recall an extraordinary case in this connection which I must relate without mentioning the names of the players concerned. These two contestants had the same score in the international tournament in question and both were sure of a prize if they drew their game. Being a bit afraid of each other they arranged beforehand that they would draw the game by seizing the first opportunity of a plausible repetition of moves. That opportunity occurred after about twenty moves, and they began to repeat a series of Bishop moves involving three different squares on either side. After these moves had been repeated twice, one of the players noticed that if he changed the order in which he occupied the three different squares concerned, and if his opponent did not change the order of his moves correspondingly, he had a rather hidden winning maneuver. The opponent did not change his order of moves because it never occurred to him even to investigate whether that order made any difference. And the reader may imagine his feelings when he was suddenly confronted by a move which did not belong in the series agreed upon and which demolished his game in short order.

Naturally, he could not complain to the tournament director that his adversary had broken an illegal agreement. And I, for one, did not waste any sympathy on him when he told me the story.

The situation is somewhat similar, when a player who has made a bad score plays one of the prospective prize-winners. While his own score may not be hurt by another loss, he would unfairly better the chances of his opponent if he did not try to win when the occasion offers itself.

I found myself involved in such a situation on occasion of the following game which was played in the U. S. National Championship tournament at Chicago, 1926. On its outcome depended the question whether or not my opponent or Marshall would win first prize while I had spoilt my own chances early in the tournament. I admired Torre's style very much and it was almost painful for me to beat him, but of course, I felt I had no choice but to play as well as I could. The game is very instructive because it shows how throughout an almost totally unexplored opening one can find his way by steadfastly adhering to the dictates of the general strategic principles.

WHITE: *Carlos Torre*   BLACK: *Edward Lasker*

1. Kt—KB3   P—Q4
2. P—B4

These two opening moves characterize the Reti Gambit. The reply P—Q5 is not likely to be good because nothing is gained by it for the development of Black's pieces. P—B3 or P—K3 could lead the game into well known paths of the Queen's Pawn opening but I wanted to avoid a closed game and preferred to test a new line of play which had been introduced by Spielmann in 1925, in the tournament at Moscow, not the least for the reason that Torre himself had participated in the Moscow tournament. I did not consider it likely that he would have expected me to choose this defense and presumed that he had rather planned and studied other variations in preparation for this game.

2. ....   P×P

3. Kt—R3

With the intention of lodging this Knight in the centre
on K5 if possible. White could, instead, turn the opening
into an accepted Queen's gambit by playing Q—R4 ch
and Q×P.

3. ....   P—K4

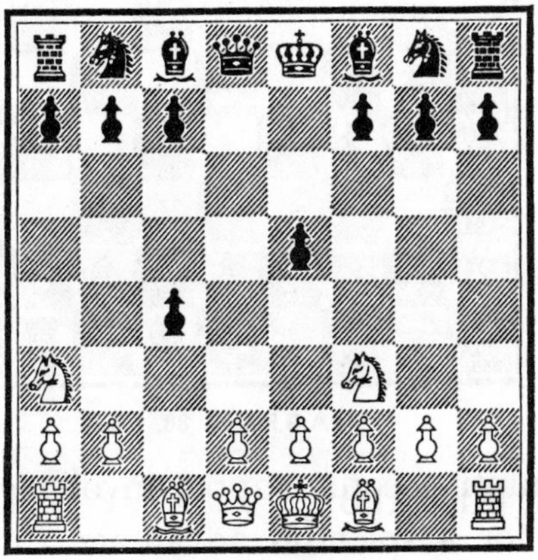

DIAGRAM 87.

This and the following three moves constitute the interesting line of play Spielmann had chosen against
Tartakower in order to produce an open game. While it
is true that Black is giving up a centre Pawn and a Bishop
for a Knight and a Pawn on the wing, he obtains a more
rapid development and attacking chances on the Queen's
side of the board. White cannot take the Bishop's Pawn
because P—K5 would drive the King's Knight back
home. On K5 he would be lost through P—KB3.

4. Kt×KP   B×Kt

5. Q—R4 ch

Of course not P×Kt, on account of Q—Q5.

5. ....   P—QKt4 !

The point of the combination. White cannot take this Pawn, as Black would win a piece through P—QB3; 7. Kt×QBP, Kt×Kt; 8. Q×Kt ch, B—Q2; 9. Q—K4 ch, B—K2.

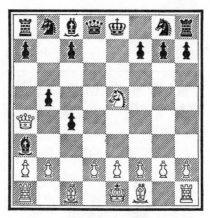

DIAGRAM 88.

A very tempting continuation, involving the sacrifice of a Pawn, for a splendid advantage in development would be 5. . . . ., Kt—Q2. Before recapturing the Bishop with the Queen White would then have to exchange Knights, and after 6. Kt×Kt, B×Kt; 7. Q×B, Kt—K2; 8. Q—QB3, O—O; Q×BP all of Black's minor pieces are developed while White has only the Queen out and must make two more Pawn moves to develop his Bishops. Black might continue with Kt—B3 or R—K.

6. Q×B   B—Kt2

To prevent Q—KB3. Tartakower in his game against Spielmann now continued with 7. P—K3, Q—Q3; 8. Q×Q, P×Q; 9. Kt—B3, Kt—QB3; 10. P—QKt3, P—Q4; 11. P×P, QP×P; 12. P—QR4 and obtained the better game through pressure on Black's QKt4 which he later in-

creased with P—Q3. My intention was to play 9. ....,
Kt—Q2 instead of QB3 in order to support the Pawn on
B5 by Kt—Kt3 in case Torre should choose the same line
of play as Tartakower. But he deviated by attacking my
Bishop's Pawn immediately.

7. P—QKt3   Q—Q3

If White now exchanges Queens, I can still lead into
the line I wanted to play. Torre pondered the position for
almost ten minutes and then made a move which, as
Marshall later pointed out, might have lost a piece for
him against two Pawns. To be frank, Marshall's rejoinder
never occurred to me. But I am not sure whether it was
not just what Torre had hoped I would play.

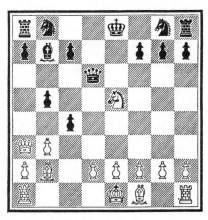

DIAGRAM 89.

8. B—Kt2 ?!   P—KB3

With P—B6 I would have won the Knight as after
9. Q×Q, P×Q two white pieces are attacked. Perhaps
White had seen the move and thought he would have
obtained a very dangerous attack with 9. P×P, Q×Kt;
10. P—QB4, Q—Kt4; 11. P—KR4, Q—R3; 12. R—R3

followed by R—K3 and Q—B5. However, 10. ....,
Q—K2 would have refuted this line of play. I did not
consider P—B6 in the game at all, but thought only of
getting my pieces developed as fast as possible. With the
text move I intended mainly to minimize the effectiveness of White's Queen's Bishop.

	9. Q×Q	P×Q
	10. Kt—B3	P×P

If in this position I had played the obvious move
Kt—Q2 which I had intended in conjunction with
Tartakower's line of development, I would have run into
trouble through 11. Kt—Q4, P—QR3; 12. P×P, P×P;
13. Kt—B5.

	11. Kt—Q4	P—QR3

Now, however, I would answer Kt—B5 with K—Q2,
and Kt×KtP would then be very dangerous for White as
after exchanging Pawns on R7 I would remain with two
connected passed Pawns.

	12. P×P	K—Q2

To keep the Knight out of my K3.

	13. Kt—B5	P—Kt3
	14. Kt—K3	

If we survey the position which has been reached after
the extended reconnoitering excursions of the white
cavalry, we must come to the conclusion that the white
army is not in very good condition. White's King's wing
is still sadly undeveloped, and as long as I control the
long diagonal with my Bishop White will have to resort
to complicated maneuvers to get his King's Bishop out.

To develop my own King's wing I need only place my King on K3 or K2, protecting my Bishop's Pawn. It is hard to decide which one of these two moves might prove

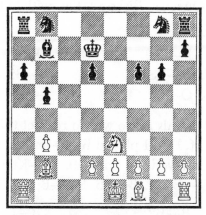

DIAGRAM 90.

more advantageous. I choose K3 because it leaves my King's Knight the choice between two moves.

14. .... K—K3
15. R—B

Threatening to invade the seventh rank, the heaven of Rooks.

15. .... Kt—QB3 ?

This gives White the opportunity for which he has been praying, to develop his King's Bishop and connect his Rooks through castling. I should have kept my Bishop unobstructed by playing Kt—Q2. There was no harm in letting White's Rook reach B7 because White could not maintain him there, due to the inability of his King's Rook to reach the Queen's Bishop's file. After 15. .... Kt—Q2; 16. R—B7, R—Kt; 17. P—B3, Kt—K2; 18.

P—Kt3, KR—QB; 19. B—R3 ch, P—B4; 20. R×R, R×R; 21. K—B2 White's King's Bishop would still have been out of play for quite a while, and I could have kept control of the Queen's Bishop's file with Kt—QB4, 22. P—QKt4, Kt—Kt6.

	16. P—Kt3	KKt—K2
	17. B—R3 ch	K—B2
	18. O—O	P—KR4

The object of this move was to restrict the mobility of White's Knight. Had I played R—Q immediately, White might have annoyed me with 19. Kt—Kt4, P—B4; 20. Kt—R6 ch, K—B; 21. B—B6, KR—B; 22. P—K4.

	19. R—B2	KR—Q
	20. KR—B	

White has now temporarily obtained control of the Queen's Bishop's file. My aim will naturally be to oppose my Rooks in that file and then to take advantage of my extra Pawn on the Queen's wing and of the weakness of White's Queen's Knight's Pawn. I felt that White could do very little to prevent this maneuver, and I thought I might as well first restrict the mobility of White's Queen's Bishop by advancing my Queen's Pawn to the fifth.

	20.	P—Q4
	21. R—B5	

Probably he did not want to block his Bishop with P—Q4 and would rather have a Pawn of mine on that square, attacked by his Bishop.

	21.	P—Q5
	22. Kt—Kt2	B—B !

Forcing the exchange of the white Bishop and thus gaining the desired Queen's Bishop's square for the Rooks.

23. B×B   QR×B
24. Kt—B4

The Knight must get back into play.

24. ....   Kt—R4 !

White can now hold the Knight's Pawn only at the expense of exchanging both Rooks, and the ending ensuing after 25. P—QKt4, Kt—Kt6; 26. R×R, R×R; 27. R×R, Kt×R was distinctly unfavorable for him due to the constant threat which the black Pawn majority on the Queen's wing constitutes. A very strong alternative I had after 25. P—QKt4 was Kt—B5. White would have had to exchange one Rook on B8 as otherwise I would exchange myself and again emerge with the two connected passed Pawns.

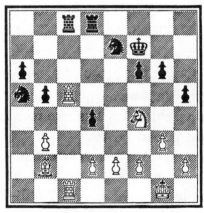

DIAGRAM 91.

The continuation might have been 26. R×R, Kt×R; 27. R—B2, Kt—K2; 28. B—B, Kt—B3; 29. Kt—Q3, R—QR and P—R4.

I was just enjoying the prospects of all these possibilities when Torre scared me for a moment with a move I had not expected at all. He played

25. R—B7 !

which sacrifices the exchange for a dangerous attack against my King. His threat is B—R3 followed by R×Kt ch and Kt×KtP. It occurred to me to play 25. ...., P—Kt5 first, leaving White's Knight's Pawn attacked. But then he could exchange Rooks and play Kt—Q3 rather than B×P, and if I took the Knight's Pawn he would take mine and I would not have the two connected passed Pawns. For this reason I dropped the idea again and concentrated upon analyzing the consequences of accepting the sacrifice. After much hard work I saw that with a counter-sacrifice I could stop the attack and regain the initiative as follows:

25.	Kt×P
26. B—R3	Kt×R
27. R×Kt ch	K—Kt
28. Kt×KtP	R—K !!

Giving up the Knight in view of the combination at my disposal on the 30th move which keeps White's King from the battle field and is thus sure to win through the advance of the passed Pawns.

White threatened various very disagreeable maneuvers. For example, if I tried the advance of the Pawns immediately, he might have played 29. R—QKt7, and if P—Kt5, 30. Kt—K7 ch. Now I would have had to give up a whole Rook to avoid a draw, for K—B; 31. Kt—Kt6 ch, K—K; 32. R—K7 would be checkmate. After 30. ...., K—B2; 31. Kt×R ch, K—K3; 32. B×P, P×B; 33. K—B !,

R×Kt; 34. R×P I could not see anything but an extremely difficult ending which I could probably not have won. Neither did 29. ...., R—Kt, 30. R—QB7, Kt×P ch; 31. K—B, P—Q6; 32. B—Kt2, threatening B×P and R—Kt7 mate seem inviting.

After the text move White has nothing better than to accept the proffered sacrifice

29.	R×R ch	R×R
30.	B×Kt	P—Q6 !

The point of the combination. White cannot take on account of R—K8 ch etc. The following ending had to be calculated with precision.

31.	P—K3	P—Kt5
32.	Kt—B4	R—Q
33.	B—Kt2	P—R4 !

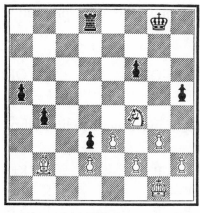

DIAGRAM 92.

It was very important not to lose a tempo by protecting the Bishop's Pawn with K—B2. In answer White could have played 34. B—Q4, P—R4; 35. Kt×P, R—QKt8; 36. B—B5, P—Kt6; 37. B—R3 or 36. ...., R—Q; 37.

B×P, P×B; 38. Kt×P, R×P; 39. Kt—B6 followed by
Kt—Q4 and I would not have been able to make any
headway.

With my Pawn on R4, however, White cannot play
B—Q4 because R×B would follow. After 35. P×R,
P—Kt6; 36. Kt×P, P—R5 one of the two Pawns would
then force his way through.

34.	B×P	R—Q2
35.	P—K4	

In order to be able to bring the Knight into play via
Q5. It would now be useless for me to play P—Kt6 as
White could stop the Pawns with B—Kt2; but the ad-
vance of Rook's Pawn deprives the Bishop of this retreat.
White now plans to give up his two pieces for my three
Pawns on the Queen's wing and then to play with four
Pawns against the Rook, which is often quite sufficient
compensation. I must therefore proceed with greatest
care.

35.	. . . .	P—QR5
36.	Kt—Q5	R—QKt2
37.	P—B3	P—R6

Now the Knight must sacrifice himself or P—Kt6 will
make a Queen.

38.	Kt×P	R×Kt
39.	K—B2	K—B2
40.	B—R8	R—Kt

The Bishop has to step very carefully. He cannot go to
R sq because R—Kt8 would win a tempo enabling him to
attack the white Pawns with R—KR8. On B3 the Bishop
would not be well placed, as P—R7 would follow and

White's King cannot take the Queen's Pawn before moving the Bishop again which I would otherwise pin with K—Kt6 and capture. For the same reason the Bishop would not be happy on Q4, where after K×P he could be

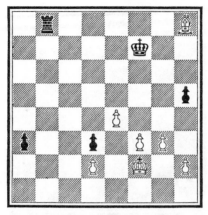

DIAGRAM 93.

pinned through R—Q. That leaves only B—K5. But even the tempo gained by this move would not have saved the game as P—R7, 42. K—K3, R—Kt8; 43. K×P, R—KR8 would have won two Pawns in short order.

41.	B—Q4	P—R7
42.	K—K3	K—Kt3
43.	P—R4	R—Kt8
44.	K×P	R—Kt8 !

This is perhaps the only move to force a clear win, a fact which apparently escaped the annotators of this game who at the time thought I was merely taking my time to enjoy myself.

After 44. . . . ., P—R8 (Q); 45. B×Q, R×B; 46. K—K3 I was unable to figure out a procedure which would permit my King to get into cooperation with the Rook and thus win one or more white Pawns and the game. The position is very difficult and requires an analysis of many variations which I did not bother going into because after my move it was practically all over.

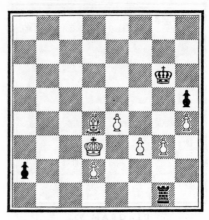

DIAGRAM 94.

45. K—K3	R×P
46. K—B4	R—R6
47. K—K5	R×BP
48. K—K6	R—Q6
49. Resigns.	

If in the position of the Diagram White had played K—B2, I would have won the Bishop by queening my Pawn and then returned to KKt8 without White's King being able to defend the Knight's Pawn.

International Chess Code

1. DEFINITION AND OBJECT

(*a*) Chess, a game in the play of which there is no element of chance, is played by two persons on a square called the Chess Board and divided into 64 squares colored light and dark alternately. Each person shall play with a series of Sixteen men, one series to be light colored and called White, and the other series to be dark colored and called Black.

(*b*) The object of the play is to checkmate the Opponent's King and the Player who checkmates thereby wins the game.

The meaning of the technical terms used in this law will be found in 3, 4 (d), 10 (a).

2. THE CHESS BOARD

(*a*) The Chess Board shall be so placed between the two persons that the nearer corner square at their respective right hands shall be light colored.

(*b*) Every vertical sequence of eight adjoining squares is termed a file.

(*c*) Every horizontal sequence of eight adjoining squares is termed a rank.

The word "diagonal" in the following Laws means a straight sequence of squares of the same color from edge to edge of the chess board and touching at angles only.

3. DESCRIPTION OF THE MEN

The men in each of the two armies are:

	Printed Symbols	
Names	WHITE	BLACK
A KING		
A QUEEN		
TWO ROOKS		
TWO BISHOPS		
TWO KNIGHTS		
EIGHT PAWNS		

4. INITIAL POSITION OF THE MEN

(*a*) The men shall be arranged on the chess board before the commencement of a game as shown in the diagram below:

BLACK

WHITE

(*b*) The first move in a game shall be made with a White man.

(*c*) The persons shall play alternately, one move at a time.

(*d*) The person whose turn it is to move is termed the Player and the other is termed the Opponent.

The technical terms "Player" and "Opponent" come into force as soon as the right to the first move has been determined.

5. NOTATION

(*a*) Only the two most widely used systems of recording chess moves, namely, the Descriptive and the Algebraic, are recognized by the F. I. D. E.

(*b*) Affiliated Units can select either of these two systems for their use.

(*c*) THE DESCRIPTIVE SYSTEM.

The men (except the Knight) are designated by their initials and the Knight by Kt. *N, if preferred, will be accepted as Kt.*

The Bishop, Knight and Rook from the King's side of the chess board are, if necessary, further designated by prefixing the letter K and the corresponding men on the Queen's side by prefixing the letter Q.

The eight files counting consecutively from left to right on the side of the chess board initially occupied by the White men are designated the QR, QKt, QB, Q, K, KB, KKt and KR files respectively.

The eight ranks are numbered for the White men 1 to 8 from the side of the chess board initially occupied by them, and inversely for the Black men 1 to 8 from the side of the chess board initially occupied by them.

A move shall be recorded by the letter designating the man moved followed by the letter or letters and number designating the file and rank respectively of the square to which the man has been moved. For instance, Q.KB4 means the Q is moved to the fourth square of the file of the King's Bishop. When two men of the same series and denomination can be moved legally to the same square, the letter or letters and number designating the file and number of the square which the moved man occupied shall be added in brackets to the letter designating the man moved. For instance R(KKt2) Kt4 means the R on the second square of the KKt file is moved to the fourth square of the same file.

If an opposing man occupy the square to which a man is moved, the designation of such opposing man shall be substituted for the designation of the square, preceded by the symbol for capture, but the latter designation, stated as from the Player's side of the chess board, shall be added in brackets if otherwise the record could be interpreted as applying to more than one opposing man.

Abbreviations

Castles KR or O—O = Castles with the KR (Short Castling).
Castles QR or O—O—O = Castles with the QR (Long Castling).
x = Captures.
Ch = Check.
Mate = Check and Mate.

(d) The ALGEBRAIC SYSTEM.

The men (except the Pawns, which are not specially indicated) are designated by the same letters as in the Descriptive System.

The eight files counting from the side of the board initially occupied by the White men and from left to right are lettered consecutively a to h.

The eight ranks counting from the same side of the board are numbered consecutively 1 to 8.

Each square is therefore named by the combination in the following order of the letter of the file and the number of the rank in which it occurs.

A move shall be recorded by the designation of the man

moved (not being a Pawn) followed by the designations respectively of the square it occupied and then the square to which it has been moved, but in abbreviated notation mention of the first-named square may be omitted unless thereby the record becomes capable of interpretation as applying to more than one man. For instance, Bc1-f4 means the Bishop on square c1 is moved to square f4 and in abbreviated notation is recorded as Bf4. A move of a Pawn shall be recorded by the combination in the following order of the letter of the file and the number of the rank in which the square to which it has been moved occurs. For instance, e7-e5 means the Pawn on square e7 is moved to square e5 and in abbreviated notation is recorded e5.

If either of two Pawns can be moved to the square named, the designation of the square which the moved Pawn occupied shall precede in brackets that of the square to which it has been moved.

Abbreviations

O—O = Castles with the KR (Short Castling)
O—O—O = Castles with the QR (Long Castling)
: or x = Captures.
+ = Check.
:+ = Captures and Checks.
± = Check and Mate.
:± = Captures and Checkmates.

Commentary Signs

! = Good move.
? = Inferior move.

6. CURRENT EXPRESSIONS

Man.—A term applicable to each King, Queen, Rook, Bishop, Knight and Pawn.

Piece.—A term applicable to each man except a Pawn.

Pinned Man.—A man that occupies a square between the King of the same color and an opposing piece that would otherwise be giving check to the King, or a man the movement of which would expose to capture a piece of a higher value than the capturing man.

Discovered Check.—Check given to the Opponent's King when the line of action of the checking piece is opened by the movement of another man of the same color.

Double Check.—Check given by the man moved in addition to the discovered check from another piece.

An Exchange.—The exchange by capture of identical men, or of men of practically the same theoretical value.

Winning or Losing the Exchange.—To exchange by capture a Bishop or Knight for a Rook is winning, and of a Rook for Bishop or Knight is losing, the Exchange.

7. MOVEMENTS OF THE MEN IN GENERAL

(*a*) and (*b*) The move of a man shall be to an unoccupied square or to a square occupied by an opposing man.

(*c*) The move of a man shall not cause such man to pass over any occupied square, except in the case of the move of the Knight.

(*d*) A legal move of a man to a square occupied by an opposing man requires the removal of that opposing man by the Player from the chess board.

8. MOVEMENTS OF THE INDIVIDUAL MEN

The King can be moved to a square adjoining the square he occupies except in the case of Castling, which is a combined move of the K and the R, but counts as one move, in which first the K, occupying his own square, is placed on one of the two nearest squares of the same color as his own in the same rank and then the R, towards which the K has been moved, is placed on the next square on the further side of the moved K. Castling is not permitted (a) when either the K or R has been moved previously; (b) when any square between the K and the R is occupied by a man; (c) if the K be in check; or (d) if Castling would cause the K to pass over, or occupy any square on which he would be in check. (See 9.)

The Queen can be moved to a square, being one of those forming the file, or the rank, or the diagonals to all of which the square the Queen occupies is common.

The Rook can be moved to a square, being one of those forming the file, or the rank, to both of which the square the R occupies is common.

The Bishop can be moved to a square, being one of those forming the diagonals to which the square the B occupies is common.

The Knight can be moved like a R one square and then like a B one square, which final square must not adjoin the square from which the Knight is moved, such movements constituting one move.

A Pawn, when not making a capture, can be moved forward on the file one or two squares on its first move, and afterwards one square only at a time.

A capture with a Pawn can be made when the opposing man occupies the nearest square forward of either of the diagonals to which the square occupied by the capturing pawn is common.

En Passant.—A Pawn which has been moved two squares on its first move is liable to be captured on the following move by a Player's Pawn that could have captured it if it had moved only one square, precisely as though it had so moved.

Promotion.—Each Pawn that is moved to a square on the eighth rank must be exchanged for a Q, R, B or Kt of the same series without regard to the number of such pieces already on the board.

9. CHECK

(*a*) and (*b*) The King is in "check" if the square he occupies is commanded by an opposing man whether pinned or not.

Note.—It is customary, but not obligatory, for the Player to advise Opponent of this fact by saying "check."

(*c*) and (*d*) The K must not be moved to a square on which he would be in "check" or to any one of the squares adjacent to the square occupied by the opposing K.

(*e*) A checked K must be moved out of check, or the checking man captured, or the check parried by the interposition of another man in the next move after the one giving check. (See 10 (*a*).)

(*f*) A Player who makes a move which does not fulfil the conditions in (*e*) must retract that move and make another move which does so comply, and, if possible, with the man he has touched in making the retracted move.

10. CHECKMATE

(*a*) Checkmate is a check from which the K cannot be relieved by any of the moves prescribed in 9 (*e*) and ends the game.

(*b*) The fact of having announced erroneously a checkmate in an indefinite or stated number of moves shall not affect the after-course of the game.

11. THE MOVE

The choice of playing the first game with the White men or the Black men shall be determined by lot, or by agreement, and in a match of two or more games the two persons shall play with the two series alternately, irrespective of the results of the games, but games annulled according to 12 shall not be reckoned in applying this rule.

12. ANNULLED GAMES

(*a*) If in the course of or *immediately* after a game it be proved that the initial position of the men on the board was incorrect, or the chess board wrongly placed initially, the game shall be annulled.

(*b*) If in the course of a game the number or position of the men be altered illegally the position immediately before the alteration occurred must be reinstated and the game resumed therefrom.

(*c*) If this position cannot be ascertained the game shall be annulled and there shall be a re-play.

13. COMPLETION OF MOVE

A move is complete:

(*a*) In moving a man from one square to another, when the Player has quitted the man.

(*b*) In capturing, when the captured man has been removed from the board and the Player has quitted the man making the capture.

(*c*) In Castling, when the Player has quitted the Rook.

(*d*) In promoting a Pawn, when the Player has replaced the Pawn by the selected piece and quitted the latter. *For sealed move see* 21.

14. ADJUSTMENT OF THE MEN

(*a*) The Player may adjust one or more of his men on their respective squares after giving previous notice of his intention so to do. (*Note.*—It is customary to use the expression "I adjust.")

(*b*) The Player shall not adjust the Opponent's men, or the Opponent the Player's men. The Opponent, however, shall adjust the position of his men on the board if requested by the Player.

(c) If the men be disarranged accidentally, the timing clocks, if in use (see 20), must be stopped immediately and the position reinstated, and, if a Tournament game, under the direction of the controlling official in charge thereof. If, moreover, it be proved either in the course of the game, or *immediately* after it is finished, that the position has been incorrectly set-up, the game shall be resumed from the correct position.

15. TOUCHING MEN

If the Player touch

(a) One of his own men he must move it.

(b) One of the Opponent's men he must take it.

(c) One of his own men and one of the Opponent's men, he must take the latter with the former, if such capture be a legal move. If not, the Opponent may require either that the Player shall move his man touched, or take with any one of his men at the Player's option with which the capture can be effected legally, the Opponent's man touched.

If none of the moves indicated in *a, b, c* can be made legally, no penalty can be exacted.

(d) Several of his own men, the Opponent has the right to name which of these men the Player shall move. If none of these men can be moved legally no penalty can be exacted.

(e) Several of the Opponent's men, the Opponent has the right to name which man shall be taken. If none of these men can be taken no penalty can be exacted.

16. DRAWN GAMES

The Game is drawn

(a) When the Player cannot make a legal move and the King is not in check. This King is then said to be stalemated.

(b) If the Player prove he can subject the Opponent's King to an endless series of checks.

(c) By recurrence of the same position three or more times, with the same player on the move, provided that either the player about to repeat the position claim the draw before completing his move, or the opponent make the claim whose turn it is to reply to a move that has repeated the position. For the purpose of this clause there shall be no distinction between King and Queen Rooks or Knights.

(d) By mutual agreement of the two players.

(e) The game shall be declared drawn if the Player prove that 50 moves have been made on each side without checkmate having been given and without any man having been captured or Pawn moved.

(f) Either the Player or the Opponent may at any period of the game demand that the other shall checkmate him in 50 moves (subject to the conditions attached in (e)). If checkmate is not given in 50 moves, the game shall be declared drawn. Nevertheless, the count of 50 moves shall begin again after each capture of any man and after each movement of a Pawn. Exception shall be made for certain positions where theoretically more than 50 moves are necessary to force a checkmate and in this case a number of moves double the number established by theory as being necessary for this object shall be allowed in lieu of the 50. The draw must be claimed by either the Player or the Opponent immediately the stipulated number of moves in Conditions (e) and/or (f) of the particular case is completed without checkmate being given, and not at any later period.

17. ILLEGAL MOVES

If a Player make an illegal move and the Opponent draw attention to the fact before touching any of his own men, the illegal move must be retracted, and the game shall be continued as follows:

(a) When a capture has not been made, the Player shall make a legal move with the man he moved illegally, but if no such legal move can be made no penalty can be exacted.

(b) If a capture has been made, the Player must either take the Opponent's man by a legal move, or make a legal move with his own man touched at the option of the Opponent, but if no such legal move can be made no penalty can be exacted.

(c) When the illegal move is a sealed move and the mistake cannot be rectified with absolute certainty by the official in charge of the game, it shall be scored as lost by the Player who sealed the illegal move.

(d) If in the course of a game it is proved that an illegal move has been made and not retracted, the position existing immediately before the illegal move was made shall be reinstated and the game shall be continued from that position. If the position cannot be reinstated the game shall be annulled.

18. PENALTIES

(a) The Opponent can exact a penalty for an infraction of these laws only if he has not touched one of his own men after the infraction occurred.

(b) Castling cannot be exacted as a penalty move.

(c) If the Opponent names as penalty a move which is illegal, his right to exact a penalty for the illegality committed by the Player shall be abrogated.

(d) Before enforcing any penalty the position which existed before the illegality occurred shall be reinstated.

19. GAMES FORFEITED

The game shall be declared forfeited by the Player or the Opponent:

(*a*) Who wilfully upsets the board or disarranges the men.

(*b*) Who refuses to resume an adjourned game within a reasonable time and in accordance with the usual regulations of Tournaments and matches.

(*c*) Who refuses to comply with a legal requirement under these laws.

(*d*) Who in the course of the game refuses to obey the rules and conform to the arrangements made for the conduct of the game.

(*e*) Who whether present or absent exceeds any time limit fixed for the consideration of his moves.

Note.—Except when unavoidably prevented the competitors in a Tournament shall conform to the directions of the official in charge.

20. THE USE OF THE CLOCK

(*a*) If the game be played with a time limit, the following rules shall apply:

1. Each competitor shall make at least 30 moves in the first two hours of his own time, 45 moves by the end of the first three similar hours, and a proportionate number of moves by the end of each successive similar hour.

2. This time limit may be modified in the regulations framed for any match or Tournament.

3. When it is proved there has been a mistake not caused by negligence in the recording of the time occupied, the mistake shall be rectified.

4. The Player is forbidden to stop his clock before completing his move except in the cases detailed in this Law.

5. When there are grounds for a claim under this Law the two clocks shall be stopped and as soon as the official in charge of the Tourna-

ment has given his decision in respect to the claim shall, if necessary, be set going again by him.

(b) If the Player exceed the time allowed for the consideration of his moves, the official in charge shall declare without making any exception the game lost by the Player (even if he and the Opponent object).

(c) If the Opponent's clock be allowed to go on, the person who notices the occurrence may not inform the Player or the Opponent but shall inform the official in charge, who shall take the necessary steps to deal with the occurrence.

(d) If a competitor in a match or a Tournament be absent at the time fixed for commencement or resumption of play, his clock shall be set going as soon as he becomes the Player, and the time which elapses until he has made his move shall count as time for the consideration of his move.

(e) The competitor who without valid reason arrives at the place of meeting more than one hour late loses the game.

(f) If both competitors without valid reason arrive at the place of meeting more than an hour late the game shall be declared lost by both.

21. ADJOURNED GAMES

(a) When a game played with or without time limit is adjourned the Player at the moment of adjournment has the right to record his move in writing.

(b) The Player must record the move himself and place it in an envelope, which he shall then seal. After affixing his signature he shall hand the envelope at once to the official in charge of the Tournament. The Player's clock, if one be in use, shall not be stopped until the record of the move is sealed.

(c) So long as the game stands adjourned neither the

Player nor the Opponent shall be allowed access to the envelope containing the sealed move.

(d) At the adjournment it shall be the duty of the Player and the Opponent to make sure that a correct record of the position as well as the time indicated as elapsed by each of the two clocks, if in use, has been recorded on the envelope.

(e) On resumption of the game it shall be the duty of the Opponent to reinstate the position on the board, set the clocks to the correct times, open the envelope, make the sealed move on the board, and finally set the Player's clock in motion.

The Player is regarded as having completed his move by sealing it and becomes the Opponent referred to in paragraph (e)

(f) The envelope containing the sealed move shall not be opened in the absence of the Player, but the official in charge shall set the Player's clock in motion at the time fixed for resumption of the game.

In paragraph (f) the Player is he whose turn it is to move after the execution of the sealed move.

(g) If the position or (in the case of a game played under the time limit) the times that have elapsed at the adjournment cannot be correctly ascertained, the game shall be annulled.

(h) If the position be reinstated incorrectly all the subsequent moves, if any, shall be annulled and the game resumed from the correct position. If the correct position cannot be ascertained, the game shall be annulled.

22. GAMES AT ODDS

(a) In a set of games, a person may give odds in all the games to the other person by giving up the right to move first.

(b) The person who receives the odds of two or more

moves must make them all at the beginning of a game in his first turn to play.

(c) If the odds consist of several moves they shall count for that number of moves in all calculation of time limit. Similarly the first move of the person who gives the odds shall count as the same number of moves as those made by the receiver of the odds.

(d) The person who receives odds of two or more moves must not move any man beyond his fourth rank until the other person has made one move.

(e) The person who gives the odds of a man or men shall have the right to move first unless such right to move is also granted.

(f) If the odds of a Pawn be given, or of a Pawn and one or more moves, the King's Bishop's Pawn shall be the Pawn removed from the board.

(g) At odds of a Rook, or a Bishop, or a Knight, the piece given is usually, and in the absence of an agreement to the contrary shall be, the Queen's piece.

(h) The person who gives the odds of a Rook may Castle as though this Rook were on the board, on the side from which the Rook has been removed, subject to the condition that this Rook's square is not occupied by any other man of either series.

23. RECORDING OF GAMES

(a) Each competitor in a match or Tournament shall record all the moves in his games in a clear and intelligible manner.

(b) In case of discrepancy between the number of moves recorded in any game by the two competitors they may stop the clocks while they are engaged in rectifying the mistake. In order to avail themselves of this right each competitor must have recorded his last move.

(*c*) The winner of a game shall give to the official in charge a correct and legible record of the game immediately on completion, and in the case of a drawn game, both players shall give in such record.

24. SUBMISSION OF DISPUTES

(*a*) A dispute on a question of fact may be submitted by agreement of the Player and Opponent to the decision of a disinterested spectator, in which case his decision shall be binding without right of appeal.

(*b*) Any question of a special nature in connection with a game, and not provided for in these Laws, or any disagreement between a Player and his Opponent as to the interpretation, or application of any of these Rules shall be submitted without delay (*a*) to an Umpire whose decision shall be given at once; (*b*) if the game is being played in a Tournament, to the governing Committee.

In both cases the game shall be adjourned until the decision is given, which decision shall be binding without right of appeal.

25. DECISION OF F. I. D. E.

The Bureau of the F. I. D. E. shall have the right to give an official, final and binding decision in any case referred to it of general doubt as to the interpretation or application of any of these Laws.

26. CONDUCT OF PLAYER AND OPPONENT

(*a*) Written or printed notes (except the record of moves made) dealing with or having any bearing on a game in progress shall not be referred to or utilized by the Player or his Opponent, and neither of them shall have recourse to any extraneous advice or information.

(*b*) No analysis of games shall be allowed in the Tournament Rooms.

(*c*) Neither Player nor Opponent shall make any comments on any of the moves in the game in progress between them.

(*d*) Neither Player nor Opponent shall touch or point to any square on the board for the purpose of facilitating reckoning possible moves.

(*e*) A legal move shall not be retracted.

(*f*) A move shall be made by transferring the man touched directly towards the square to be occupied, and the man must be quitted immediately it has been placed on that square.

In Castling the King shall first be moved and afterwards the Rook.

In promoting a Pawn the Player shall immediately remove the Pawn from the Board and place the substituted piece on the vacated square.

In Capturing, the Player shall immediately remove the captured man from the board.

(*g*) No comments of any kind, or suggestions as to drawing or abandoning the game shall be added to a sealed move.

(*h*) The Player who perceives that his Opponent's clock is going should call his attention to the fact.

(*i*) Neither Player nor Opponent shall in any way whatsoever distract the attention of, or cause annoyance to, the other.

A CATALOG OF SELECTED
DOVER BOOKS
IN ALL FIELDS OF INTEREST

A CATALOG OF SELECTED
DOVER BOOKS
IN ALL FIELDS OF INTEREST

DRAWINGS OF REMBRANDT, edited by Seymour Slive. Updated Lippmann, Hofstede de Groot edition, with definitive scholarly apparatus. All portraits, biblical sketches, landscapes, nudes. Oriental figures, classical studies, together with selection of work by followers. 550 illustrations. Total of 630pp. 9⅛ × 12¼.
21485-0, 21486-9 Pa., Two-vol. set $29.90

GHOST AND HORROR STORIES OF AMBROSE BIERCE, Ambrose Bierce. 24 tales vividly imagined, strangely prophetic, and decades ahead of their time in technical skill: "The Damned Thing," "An Inhabitant of Carcosa," "The Eyes of the Panther," "Moxon's Master," and 20 more. 199pp. 5⅜ × 8½. 20767-6 Pa. $4.95

ETHICAL WRITINGS OF MAIMONIDES, Maimonides. Most significant ethical works of great medieval sage, newly translated for utmost precision, readability. Laws Concerning Character Traits, Eight Chapters, more. 192pp. 5⅜ × 8½.
24522-5 Pa. $5.95

THE EXPLORATION OF THE COLORADO RIVER AND ITS CANYONS, J. W. Powell. Full text of Powell's 1,000-mile expedition down the fabled Colorado in 1869. Superb account of terrain, geology, vegetation, Indians, famine, mutiny, treacherous rapids, mighty canyons, during exploration of last unknown part of continental U.S. 400pp. 5⅜ × 8½. 20094-9 Pa. $7.95

HISTORY OF PHILOSOPHY, Julián Marías. Clearest one-volume history on the market. Every major philosopher and dozens of others, to Existentialism and later. 505pp. 5⅜ × 8½. 21739-6 Pa. $9.95

ALL ABOUT LIGHTNING, Martin A. Uman. Highly readable nontechnical survey of nature and causes of lightning, thunderstorms, ball lightning, St. Elmo's Fire, much more. Illustrated. 192pp. 5⅜ × 8½. 25237-X Pa. $5.95

SAILING ALONE AROUND THE WORLD, Captain Joshua Slocum. First man to sail around the world, alone, in small boat. One of great feats of seamanship told in delightful manner. 67 illustrations. 294pp. 5⅜ × 8½. 20326-3 Pa. $4.95

LETTERS AND NOTES ON THE MANNERS, CUSTOMS AND CONDITIONS OF THE NORTH AMERICAN INDIANS, George Catlin. Classic account of life among Plains Indians: ceremonies, hunt, warfare, etc. 312 plates. 572pp. of text. 6⅛ × 9¼. 22118-0, 22119-9, Pa., Two-vol. set $17.90

THE SECRET LIFE OF SALVADOR DALÍ, Salvador Dalí. Outrageous but fascinating autobiography through Dalí's thirties with scores of drawings and sketches and 80 photographs. A must for lovers of 20th-century art. 432pp. 6½ × 9¼. (Available in U.S. only) 27454-3 Pa. $9.95

THE BOOK OF BEASTS: Being a Translation from a Latin Bestiary of the Twelfth Century, T. H. White. Wonderful catalog of real and fanciful beasts: manticore, griffin, phoenix, amphivius, jaculus, many more. White's witty erudite commentary on scientific, historical aspects enhances fascinating glimpse of medieval mind. Illustrated. 296pp. 5⅜ × 8¼. (Available in U.S. only) 24609-4 Pa. $7.95

FRANK LLOYD WRIGHT: Architecture and Nature with 160 Illustrations, Donald Hoffmann. Profusely illustrated study of influence of nature—especially prairie—on Wright's designs for Fallingwater, Robie House, Guggenheim Museum, other masterpieces. 96pp. 9¼ × 10¾. 25098-9 Pa. $8.95

FRANK LLOYD WRIGHT'S FALLINGWATER, Donald Hoffmann. Wright's famous waterfall house: planning and construction of organic idea. History of site, owners, Wright's personal involvement. Photographs of various stages of building. Preface by Edgar Kaufmann, Jr. 100 illustrations. 112pp. 9¼ × 10. 23671-4 Pa. $8.95

YEARS WITH FRANK LLOYD WRIGHT: Apprentice to Genius, Edgar Tafel. Insightful memoir by a former apprentice presents a revealing portrait of Wright the man, the inspired teacher, the greatest American architect. 372 black-and-white illustrations. Preface. Index. vi + 228pp. 8¼ × 11. 24801-1 Pa. $10.95

THE STORY OF KING ARTHUR AND HIS KNIGHTS, Howard Pyle. Enchanting version of King Arthur fable has delighted generations with imaginative narratives of exciting adventures and unforgettable illustrations by the author. 41 illustrations. xviii + 313pp. 6⅛ × 9¼. 21445-1 Pa. $6.95

THE GODS OF THE EGYPTIANS, E. A. Wallis Budge. Thorough coverage of numerous gods of ancient Egypt by foremost Egyptologist. Information on evolution of cults, rites and gods; the cult of Osiris; the Book of the Dead and its rites; the sacred animals and birds; Heaven and Hell; and more. 956pp. 6⅛ × 9¼. 22055-9, 22056-7 Pa., Two-vol. set $21.90

A THEOLOGICO-POLITICAL TREATISE, Benedict Spinoza. Also contains unfinished *Political Treatise*. Great classic on religious liberty, theory of government on common consent. R. Elwes translation. Total of 421pp. 5⅜ × 8½. 20249-6 Pa. $7.95

INCIDENTS OF TRAVEL IN CENTRAL AMERICA, CHIAPAS, AND YUCATAN, John L. Stephens. Almost single-handed discovery of Maya culture; exploration of ruined cities, monuments, temples; customs of Indians. 115 drawings. 892pp. 5⅜ × 8½. 22404-X, 22405-8 Pa., Two-vol. set $17.90

LOS CAPRICHOS, Francisco Goya. 80 plates of wild, grotesque monsters and caricatures. Prado manuscript included. 183pp. 6⅜ × 9⅜. 22384-1 Pa. $6.95

AUTOBIOGRAPHY: The Story of My Experiments with Truth, Mohandas K. Gandhi. Not hagiography, but Gandhi in his own words. Boyhood, legal studies, purification, the growth of the Satyagraha (nonviolent protest) movement. Critical, inspiring work of the man who freed India. 480pp. 5⅜ × 8½. (Available in U.S. only) 24593-4 Pa. $6.95

ILLUSTRATED DICTIONARY OF HISTORIC ARCHITECTURE, edited by Cyril M. Harris. Extraordinary compendium of clear, concise definitions for over 5,000 important architectural terms complemented by over 2,000 line drawings. Covers full spectrum of architecture from ancient ruins to 20th-century Modernism. Preface. 592pp. 7½ × 9⅝. 24444-X Pa. $15.95

THE NIGHT BEFORE CHRISTMAS, Clement Moore. Full text, and woodcuts from original 1848 book. Also critical, historical material. 19 illustrations. 40pp. 4⅝ × 6. 22797-9 Pa. $2.50

THE LESSON OF JAPANESE ARCHITECTURE: 165 Photographs, Jiro Harada. Memorable gallery of 165 photographs taken in the 1930's of exquisite Japanese homes of the well-to-do and historic buildings. 13 line diagrams. 192pp. 8⅜ × 11¼. 24778-3 Pa. $10.95

THE AUTOBIOGRAPHY OF CHARLES DARWIN AND SELECTED LETTERS, edited by Francis Darwin. The fascinating life of eccentric genius composed of an intimate memoir by Darwin (intended for his children); commentary by his son, Francis; hundreds of fragments from notebooks, journals, papers; and letters to and from Lyell, Hooker, Huxley, Wallace and Henslow. xi + 365pp. 5⅜ × 8. 20479-0 Pa. $6.95

WONDERS OF THE SKY: Observing Rainbows, Comets, Eclipses, the Stars and Other Phenomena, Fred Schaaf. Charming, easy-to-read poetic guide to all manner of celestial events visible to the naked eye. Mock suns, glories, Belt of Venus, more. Illustrated. 299pp. 5¼ × 8¼. 24402-4 Pa. $7.95

BURNHAM'S CELESTIAL HANDBOOK, Robert Burnham, Jr. Thorough guide to the stars beyond our solar system. Exhaustive treatment. Alphabetical by constellation: Andromeda to Cetus in Vol. 1; Chamaeleon to Orion in Vol. 2; and Pavo to Vulpecula in Vol. 3. Hundreds of illustrations. Index in Vol. 3. 2,000pp. 6⅛ × 9¼. 23567-X, 23568-8, 23673-0 Pa., Three-vol. set $41.85

STAR NAMES: Their Lore and Meaning, Richard Hinckley Allen. Fascinating history of names various cultures have given to constellations and literary and folkloristic uses that have been made of stars. Indexes to subjects. Arabic and Greek names. Biblical references. Bibliography. 563pp. 5⅜ × 8½. 21079-0 Pa. $8.95

THIRTY YEARS THAT SHOOK PHYSICS: The Story of Quantum Theory, George Gamow. Lucid, accessible introduction to influential theory of energy and matter. Careful explanations of Dirac's anti-particles, Bohr's model of the atom, much more. 12 plates. Numerous drawings. 240pp. 5⅜ × 8½. 24895-X Pa. $5.95

CHINESE DOMESTIC FURNITURE IN PHOTOGRAPHS AND MEASURED DRAWINGS, Gustav Ecke. A rare volume, now affordably priced for antique collectors, furniture buffs and art historians. Detailed review of styles ranging from early Shang to late Ming. Unabridged republication. 161 black-and-white drawings, photos. Total of 224pp. 8⅜ × 11¼. (Available in U.S. only) 25171-3 Pa. $13.95

VINCENT VAN GOGH: A Biography, Julius Meier-Graefe. Dynamic, penetrating study of artist's life, relationship with brother, Theo, painting techniques, travels, more. Readable, engrossing. 160pp. 5⅜ × 8½. (Available in U.S. only) 25253-1 Pa. $4.95

HOW TO WRITE, Gertrude Stein. Gertrude Stein claimed anyone could understand her unconventional writing—here are clues to help. Fascinating improvisations, language experiments, explanations illuminate Stein's craft and the art of writing. Total of 414pp. 4⅝ × 6⅜.   23144-5 Pa. $6.95

ADVENTURES AT SEA IN THE GREAT AGE OF SAIL: Five Firsthand Narratives, edited by Elliot Snow. Rare true accounts of exploration, whaling, shipwreck, fierce natives, trade, shipboard life, more. 33 illustrations. Introduction. 353pp. 5⅜ × 8½.   25177-2 Pa. $8.95

THE HERBAL OR GENERAL HISTORY OF PLANTS, John Gerard. Classic descriptions of about 2,850 plants—with over 2,700 illustrations—includes Latin and English names, physical descriptions, varieties, time and place of growth, more. 2,706 illustrations. xlv + 1,678pp. 8½ × 12¼.   23147-X Cloth. $75.00

DOROTHY AND THE WIZARD IN OZ, L. Frank Baum. Dorothy and the Wizard visit the center of the Earth, where people are vegetables, glass houses grow and Oz characters reappear. Classic sequel to *Wizard of Oz*. 256pp. 5⅜ × 8.
24714-7 Pa. $5.95

SONGS OF EXPERIENCE: Facsimile Reproduction with 26 Plates in Full Color, William Blake. This facsimile of Blake's original "Illuminated Book" reproduces 26 full-color plates from a rare 1826 edition. Includes "The Tyger," "London," "Holy Thursday," and other immortal poems. 26 color plates. Printed text of poems. 48pp. 5¼ × 7.   24636-1 Pa. $3.95

SONGS OF INNOCENCE, William Blake. The first and most popular of Blake's famous "Illuminated Books," in a facsimile edition reproducing all 31 brightly colored plates. Additional printed text of each poem. 64pp. 5¼ × 7.
22764-2 Pa. $3.95

PRECIOUS STONES, Max Bauer. Classic, thorough study of diamonds, rubies, emeralds, garnets, etc.: physical character, occurrence, properties, use, similar topics. 20 plates, 8 in color. 94 figures. 659pp. 6⅛ × 9¼.
21910-0, 21911-9 Pa., Two-vol. set $15.90

ENCYCLOPEDIA OF VICTORIAN NEEDLEWORK, S. F. A. Caulfeild and Blanche Saward. Full, precise descriptions of stitches, techniques for dozens of needlecrafts—most exhaustive reference of its kind. Over 800 figures. Total of 679pp. 8⅛ × 11. Two volumes.   Vol. 1 22800-2 Pa. $11.95
Vol. 2 22801-0 Pa. $11.95

THE MARVELOUS LAND OF OZ, L. Frank Baum. Second Oz book, the Scarecrow and Tin Woodman are back with hero named Tip, Oz magic. 136 illustrations. 287pp. 5⅜ × 8½.   20692-0 Pa. $5.95

WILD FOWL DECOYS, Joel Barber. Basic book on the subject, by foremost authority and collector. Reveals history of decoy making and rigging, place in American culture, different kinds of decoys, how to make them, and how to use them. 140 plates. 156pp. 7⅞ × 10¾.   20011-6 Pa. $8.95

HISTORY OF LACE, Mrs. Bury Palliser. Definitive, profusely illustrated chronicle of lace from earliest times to late 19th century. Laces of Italy, Greece, England, France, Belgium, etc. Landmark of needlework scholarship. 266 illustrations. 672pp. 6⅛ × 9¼.   24742-2 Pa. $14.95

ILLUSTRATED GUIDE TO SHAKER FURNITURE, Robert Meader. All furniture and appurtenances, with much on unknown local styles. 235 photos. 146pp. 9 × 12. 22819-3 Pa. $8.95

WHALE SHIPS AND WHALING: A Pictorial Survey, George Francis Dow. Over 200 vintage engravings, drawings, photographs of barks, brigs, cutters, other vessels. Also harpoons, lances, whaling guns, many other artifacts. Comprehensive text by foremost authority. 207 black-and-white illustrations. 288pp. 6 × 9. 24808-9 Pa. $9.95

THE BERTRAMS, Anthony Trollope. Powerful portrayal of blind self-will and thwarted ambition includes one of Trollope's most heartrending love stories. 497pp. 5⅜ × 8½. 25119-5 Pa. $9.95

ADVENTURES WITH A HAND LENS, Richard Headstrom. Clearly written guide to observing and studying flowers and grasses, fish scales, moth and insect wings, egg cases, buds, feathers, seeds, leaf scars, moss, molds, ferns, common crystals, etc.—all with an ordinary, inexpensive magnifying glass. 209 exact line drawings aid in your discoveries. 220pp. 5⅜ × 8½. 23330-8 Pa. $4.95

RODIN ON ART AND ARTISTS, Auguste Rodin. Great sculptor's candid, wide-ranging comments on meaning of art; great artists; relation of sculpture to poetry, painting, music; philosophy of life, more. 76 superb black-and-white illustrations of Rodin's sculpture, drawings and prints. 119pp. 8⅜ × 11¼. 24487-3 Pa. $7.95

FIFTY CLASSIC FRENCH FILMS, 1912–1982: A Pictorial Record, Anthony Slide. Memorable stills from Grand Illusion, Beauty and the Beast, Hiroshima, Mon Amour, many more. Credits, plot synopses, reviews, etc. 160pp. 8¼ × 11. 25256-6 Pa. $11.95

THE PRINCIPLES OF PSYCHOLOGY, William James. Famous long course complete, unabridged. Stream of thought, time perception, memory, experimental methods; great work decades ahead of its time. 94 figures. 1,391pp. 5⅜ × 8½. 20381-6, 20382-4 Pa., Two-vol. set $23.90

BODIES IN A BOOKSHOP, R. T. Campbell. Challenging mystery of blackmail and murder with ingenious plot and superbly drawn characters. In the best tradition of British suspense fiction. 192pp. 5⅜ × 8½. 24720-1 Pa. $4.95

CALLAS: PORTRAIT OF A PRIMA DONNA, George Jellinek. Renowned commentator on the musical scene chronicles incredible career and life of the most controversial, fascinating, influential operatic personality of our time. 64 black-and-white photographs. 416pp. 5⅜ × 8¼. 25047-4 Pa. $8.95

GEOMETRY, RELATIVITY AND THE FOURTH DIMENSION, Rudolph Rucker. Exposition of fourth dimension, concepts of relativity as Flatland characters continue adventures. Popular, easily followed yet accurate, profound. 141 illustrations. 133pp. 5⅜ × 8½. 23400-2 Pa. $4.95

HOUSEHOLD STORIES BY THE BROTHERS GRIMM, with pictures by Walter Crane. 53 classic stories—Rumpelstiltskin, Rapunzel, Hansel and Gretel, the Fisherman and his Wife, Snow White, Tom Thumb, Sleeping Beauty, Cinderella, and so much more—lavishly illustrated with original 19th century drawings. 114 illustrations. x + 269pp. 5⅜ × 8½. 21080-4 Pa. $4.95

SUNDIALS, Albert Waugh. Far and away the best, most thorough coverage of ideas, mathematics concerned, types, construction, adjusting anywhere. Over 100 illustrations. 230pp. 5⅜ × 8½. 22947-5 Pa. $5.95

PICTURE HISTORY OF THE NORMANDIE: With 190 Illustrations, Frank O. Braynard. Full story of legendary French ocean liner: Art Deco interiors, design innovations, furnishings, celebrities, maiden voyage, tragic fire, much more. Extensive text. 144pp. 8⅞ × 11¼. 25257-4 Pa. $10.95

THE FIRST AMERICAN COOKBOOK: A Facsimile of "American Cookery," 1796, Amelia Simmons. Facsimile of the first American-written cookbook published in the United States contains authentic recipes for colonial favorites— pumpkin pudding, winter squash pudding, spruce beer, Indian slapjacks, and more. Introductory Essay and Glossary of colonial cooking terms. 80pp. 5⅜ × 8½. 24710-4 Pa. $3.50

101 PUZZLES IN THOUGHT AND LOGIC, C. R. Wylie, Jr. Solve murders and robberies, find out which fishermen are liars, how a blind man could possibly identify a color—purely by your own reasoning! 107pp. 5⅜ × 8½. 20367-0 Pa. $2.95

ANCIENT EGYPTIAN MYTHS AND LEGENDS, Lewis Spence. Examines animism, totemism, fetishism, creation myths, deities, alchemy, art and magic, other topics. Over 50 illustrations. 432pp. 5⅜ × 8½. 26525-0 Pa. $8.95

ANTHROPOLOGY AND MODERN LIFE, Franz Boas. Great anthropologist's classic treatise on race and culture. Introduction by Ruth Bunzel. Only inexpensive paperback edition. 255pp. 5⅜ × 8½. 25245-0 Pa. $7.95

THE TALE OF PETER RABBIT, Beatrix Potter. The inimitable Peter's terrifying adventure in Mr. McGregor's garden, with all 27 wonderful, full-color Potter illustrations. 55pp. 4¼ × 5½. (Available in U.S. only) 22827-4 Pa. $1.75

THREE PROPHETIC SCIENCE FICTION NOVELS, H. G. Wells. *When the Sleeper Wakes, A Story of the Days to Come* and *The Time Machine* (full version). 335pp. 5⅜ × 8½. (Available in U.S. only) 20605-X Pa. $8.95

APICIUS COOKERY AND DINING IN IMPERIAL ROME, edited and translated by Joseph Dommers Vehling. Oldest known cookbook in existence offers readers a clear picture of what foods Romans ate, how they prepared them, etc. 49 illustrations. 301pp. 6⅛ × 9¼. 23563-7 Pa. $7.95

SHAKESPEARE LEXICON AND QUOTATION DICTIONARY, Alexander Schmidt. Full definitions, locations, shades of meaning of every word in plays and poems. More than 50,000 exact quotations. 1,485pp. 6½ × 9¼. 22726-X, 22727-8 Pa., Two-vol. set $31.90

THE WORLD'S GREAT SPEECHES, edited by Lewis Copeland and Lawrence W. Lamm. Vast collection of 278 speeches from Greeks to 1970. Powerful and effective models; unique look at history. 842pp. 5⅜ × 8½. 20468-5 Pa. $12.95

THE BLUE FAIRY BOOK, Andrew Lang. The first, most famous collection, with many familiar tales: Little Red Riding Hood, Aladdin and the Wonderful Lamp, Puss in Boots, Sleeping Beauty, Hansel and Gretel, Rumpelstiltskin; 37 in all. 138 illustrations. 390pp. 5⅜ × 8½.   21437-0 Pa. $6.95

THE STORY OF THE CHAMPIONS OF THE ROUND TABLE, Howard Pyle. Sir Launcelot, Sir Tristram and Sir Percival in spirited adventures of love and triumph retold in Pyle's inimitable style. 50 drawings, 31 full-page. xviii + 329pp. 6½ × 9¼.   21883-X Pa. $7.95

THE MYTHS OF THE NORTH AMERICAN INDIANS, Lewis Spence. Myths and legends of the Algonquins, Iroquois, Pawnees and Sioux with comprehensive historical and ethnological commentary. 36 illustrations. 5⅜ × 8½.
25967-6 Pa. $8.95

GREAT DINOSAUR HUNTERS AND THEIR DISCOVERIES, Edwin H. Colbert. Fascinating, lavishly illustrated chronicle of dinosaur research, 1820s to 1960. Achievements of Cope, Marsh, Brown, Buckland, Mantell, Huxley, many others. 384pp. 5¼ × 8¼.   24701-5 Pa. $7.95

THE TASTEMAKERS, Russell Lynes. Informal, illustrated social history of American taste 1850s–1950s. First popularized categories Highbrow, Lowbrow, Middlebrow. 129 illustrations. New (1979) afterword. 384pp. 6 × 9.
23993-4 Pa. $8.95

DOUBLE CROSS PURPOSES, Ronald A. Knox. A treasure hunt in the Scottish Highlands, an old map, unidentified corpse, surprise discoveries keep reader guessing in this cleverly intricate tale of financial skullduggery. 2 black-and-white maps. 320pp. 5⅜ × 8½. (Available in U.S. only)   25032-6 Pa. $6.95

AUTHENTIC VICTORIAN DECORATION AND ORNAMENTATION IN FULL COLOR: 46 Plates from "Studies in Design," Christopher Dresser. Superb full-color lithographs reproduced from rare original portfolio of a major Victorian designer. 48pp. 9¼ × 12¼.   25083-0 Pa. $7.95

PRIMITIVE ART, Franz Boas. Remains the best text ever prepared on subject, thoroughly discussing Indian, African, Asian, Australian, and, especially, Northern American primitive art. Over 950 illustrations show ceramics, masks, totem poles, weapons, textiles, paintings, much more. 376pp. 5⅜ × 8.   20025-6 Pa. $7.95

SIDELIGHTS ON RELATIVITY, Albert Einstein. Unabridged republication of two lectures delivered by the great physicist in 1920–21. *Ether and Relativity* and *Geometry and Experience*. Elegant ideas in nonmathematical form, accessible to intelligent layman. vi + 56pp. 5⅜ × 8½.   24511-X Pa. $3.95

THE WIT AND HUMOR OF OSCAR WILDE, edited by Alvin Redman. More than 1,000 ripostes, paradoxes, wisecracks: Work is the curse of the drinking classes, I can resist everything except temptation, etc. 258pp. 5⅜ × 8½.   20602-5 Pa. $4.95

ADVENTURES WITH A MICROSCOPE, Richard Headstrom. 59 adventures with clothing fibers, protozoa, ferns and lichens, roots and leaves, much more. 142 illustrations. 232pp. 5⅜ × 8½.   23471-1 Pa. $4.95

PLANTS OF THE BIBLE, Harold N. Moldenke and Alma L. Moldenke. Standard reference to all 230 plants mentioned in Scriptures. Latin name, biblical reference, uses, modern identity, much more. Unsurpassed encyclopedic resource for scholars, botanists, nature lovers, students of Bible. Bibliography. Indexes. 123 black-and-white illustrations. 384pp. 6 × 9. 25069-5 Pa. $8.95

FAMOUS AMERICAN WOMEN: A Biographical Dictionary from Colonial Times to the Present, Robert McHenry, ed. From Pocahontas to Rosa Parks, 1,035 distinguished American women documented in separate biographical entries. Accurate, up-to-date data, numerous categories, spans 400 years. Indices. 493pp. 6½ × 9¼. 24523-3 Pa. $10.95

THE FABULOUS INTERIORS OF THE GREAT OCEAN LINERS IN HIS-TORIC PHOTOGRAPHS, William H. Miller, Jr. Some 200 superb photographs capture exquisite interiors of world's great "floating palaces"—1890s to 1980s: *Titanic, Ile de France, Queen Elizabeth, United States, Europa*, more. Approx. 200 black-and-white photographs. Captions. Text. Introduction. 160pp. 8⅞ × 11¼. 24756-2 Pa. $9.95

THE GREAT LUXURY LINERS, 1927-1954: A Photographic Record, William H. Miller, Jr. Nostalgic tribute to heyday of ocean liners. 186 photos of *Ile de France, Normandie, Leviathan, Queen Elizabeth, United States*, many others. Interior and exterior views. Introduction. Captions. 160pp. 9 × 12. 24056-8 Pa. $12.95

A NATURAL HISTORY OF THE DUCKS, John Charles Phillips. Great landmark of ornithology offers complete detailed coverage of nearly 200 species and subspecies of ducks: gadwall, sheldrake, merganser, pintail, many more. 74 full-color plates, 102 black-and-white. Bibliography. Total of 1,920pp. 8⅜ × 11¼. 25141-1, 25142-X Cloth., Two-vol. set $100.00

THE SEAWEED HANDBOOK: An Illustrated Guide to Seaweeds from North Carolina to Canada, Thomas F. Lee. Concise reference covers 78 species. Scientific and common names, habitat, distribution, more. Finding keys for easy identification. 224pp. 5⅜ × 8½. 25215-9 Pa. $6.95

THE TEN BOOKS OF ARCHITECTURE: The 1755 Leoni Edition, Leon Battista Alberti. Rare classic helped introduce the glories of ancient architecture to the Renaissance. 68 black-and-white plates. 336pp. 8⅜ × 11¼. 25239-6 Pa. $14.95

MISS MACKENZIE, Anthony Trollope. Minor masterpieces by Victorian master unmasks many truths about life in 19th-century England. First inexpensive edition in years. 392pp. 5⅜ × 8½. 25201-9 Pa. $8.95

THE RIME OF THE ANCIENT MARINER, Gustave Doré, Samuel Taylor Coleridge. Dramatic engravings considered by many to be his greatest work. The terrifying space of the open sea, the storms and whirlpools of an unknown ocean, the ice of Antarctica, more—all rendered in a powerful, chilling manner. Full text. 38 plates. 77pp. 9¼ × 12. 22305-1 Pa. $4.95

THE EXPEDITIONS OF ZEBULON MONTGOMERY PIKE, Zebulon Montgomery Pike. Fascinating firsthand accounts (1805-6) of exploration of Mississippi River, Indian wars, capture by Spanish dragoons, much more. 1,088pp. 5⅜ × 8½. 25254-X, 25255-8 Pa., Two-vol. set $25.90

A CONCISE HISTORY OF PHOTOGRAPHY: Third Revised Edition, Helmut Gernsheim. Best one-volume history—camera obscura, photochemistry, daguerreotypes, evolution of cameras, film, more. Also artistic aspects—landscape, portraits, fine art, etc. 281 black-and-white photographs. 26 in color. 176pp. 8⅜ × 11¼.
25128-4 Pa. $14.95

THE DORÉ BIBLE ILLUSTRATIONS, Gustave Doré. 241 detailed plates from the Bible: the Creation scenes, Adam and Eve, Flood, Babylon, battle sequences, life of Jesus, etc. Each plate is accompanied by the verses from the King James version of the Bible. 241pp. 9 × 12.
23004-X Pa. $9.95

WANDERINGS IN WEST AFRICA, Richard F. Burton. Great Victorian scholar/adventurer's invaluable descriptions of African tribal rituals, fetishism, culture, art, much more. Fascinating 19th-century account. 624pp. 5⅜ × 8½. 26890-X Pa. $12.95

HISTORIC HOMES OF THE AMERICAN PRESIDENTS, Second Revised Edition, Irvin Haas. Guide to homes occupied by every president from Washington to Bush. Visiting hours, travel routes, more. 175 photos. 160pp. 8¼ × 11.
26751-2 Pa. $9.95

THE HISTORY OF THE LEWIS AND CLARK EXPEDITION, Meriwether Lewis and William Clark, edited by Elliott Coues. Classic edition of Lewis and Clark's day-by-day journals that later became the basis for U.S. claims to Oregon and the West. Accurate and invaluable geographical, botanical, biological, meteorological and anthropological material. Total of 1,508pp. 5⅜ × 8½.
21268-8, 21269-6, 21270-X Pa., Three-vol. set $29.85

LANGUAGE, TRUTH AND LOGIC, Alfred J. Ayer. Famous, clear introduction to Vienna, Cambridge schools of Logical Positivism. Role of philosophy, elimination of metaphysics, nature of analysis, etc. 160pp. 5⅜ × 8½. (Available in U.S. and Canada only)
20010-8 Pa. $3.95

MATHEMATICS FOR THE NONMATHEMATICIAN, Morris Kline. Detailed, college-level treatment of mathematics in cultural and historical context, with numerous exercises. For liberal arts students. Preface. Recommended Reading Lists. Tables. Index. Numerous black-and-white figures. xvi + 641pp. 5⅜ × 8½.
24823-2 Pa. $11.95

HANDBOOK OF PICTORIAL SYMBOLS, Rudolph Modley. 3,250 signs and symbols, many systems in full; official or heavy commercial use. Arranged by subject. Most in Pictorial Archive series. 143pp. 8⅛ × 11. 23357-X Pa. $7.95

INCIDENTS OF TRAVEL IN YUCATAN, John L. Stephens. Classic (1843) exploration of jungles of Yucatan, looking for evidences of Maya civilization. Travel adventures, Mexican and Indian culture, etc. Total of 669pp. 5⅜ × 8½.
20926-1, 20927-X Pa., Two-vol. set $13.90

CATALOG OF DOVER BOOKS

DEGAS: An Intimate Portrait, Ambroise Vollard. Charming, anecdotal memoir by famous art dealer of one of the greatest 19th-century French painters. 14 black-and-white illustrations. Introduction by Harold L. Van Doren. 96pp. 5⅜ × 8½.
25131-4 Pa. $4.95

PERSONAL NARRATIVE OF A PILGRIMAGE TO AL-MADINAH AND MECCAH, Richard F. Burton. Great travel classic by remarkably colorful personality. Burton, disguised as a Moroccan, visited sacred shrines of Islam, narrowly escaping death. 47 illustrations. 959pp. 5⅜ × 8½.
21217-3, 21218-1 Pa., Two-vol. set $19.90

PHRASE AND WORD ORIGINS, A. H. Holt. Entertaining, reliable, modern study of more than 1,200 colorful words, phrases, origins and histories. Much unexpected information. 254pp. 5⅜ × 8½.
20758-7 Pa. $5.95

THE RED THUMB MARK, R. Austin Freeman. In this first Dr. Thorndyke case, the great scientific detective draws fascinating conclusions from the nature of a single fingerprint. Exciting story, authentic science. 320pp. 5⅜ × 8½. (Available in U.S. only)
25210-8 Pa. $6.95

AN EGYPTIAN HIEROGLYPHIC DICTIONARY, E. A. Wallis Budge. Monumental work containing about 25,000 words or terms that occur in texts ranging from 3000 B.C. to 600 A.D. Each entry consists of a transliteration of the word, the word in hieroglyphs, and the meaning in English. 1,314pp. 6⅜ × 10.
23615-3, 23616-1 Pa., Two-vol. set $35.90

THE COMPLEAT STRATEGYST: Being a Primer on the Theory of Games of Strategy, J. D. Williams. Highly entertaining classic describes, with many illustrated examples, how to select best strategies in conflict situations. Prefaces. Appendices. xvi + 268pp. 5⅜ × 8½.
25101-2 Pa. $6.95

THE ROAD TO OZ, L. Frank Baum. Dorothy meets the Shaggy Man, little Button-Bright and the Rainbow's beautiful daughter in this delightful trip to the magical Land of Oz. 272pp. 5⅜ × 8.
25208-6 Pa. $5.95

POINT AND LINE TO PLANE, Wassily Kandinsky. Seminal exposition of role of point, line, other elements in nonobjective painting. Essential to understanding 20th-century art. 127 illustrations. 192pp. 6½ × 9¼.
23808-3 Pa. $5.95

LADY ANNA, Anthony Trollope. Moving chronicle of Countess Lovel's bitter struggle to win for herself and daughter Anna their rightful rank and fortune—perhaps at cost of sanity itself. 384pp. 5⅜ × 8½.
24669-8 Pa. $8.95

EGYPTIAN MAGIC, E. A. Wallis Budge. Sums up all that is known about magic in Ancient Egypt: the role of magic in controlling the gods, powerful amulets that warded off evil spirits, scarabs of immortality, use of wax images, formulas and spells, the secret name, much more. 253pp. 5⅜ × 8½.
22681-6 Pa. $4.95

THE DANCE OF SIVA, Ananda Coomaraswamy. Preeminent authority unfolds the vast metaphysic of India: the revelation of her art, conception of the universe, social organization, etc. 27 reproductions of art masterpieces. 192pp. 5⅜ × 8½.
24817-8 Pa. $6.95

CATALOG OF DOVER BOOKS

CHRISTMAS CUSTOMS AND TRADITIONS, Clement A. Miles. Origin, evolution, significance of religious, secular practices. Caroling, gifts, yule logs, much more. Full, scholarly yet fascinating; non-sectarian. 400pp. 5⅜ × 8½.
23354-5 Pa. $7.95

THE HUMAN FIGURE IN MOTION, Eadweard Muybridge. More than 4,500 stopped-action photos, in action series, showing undraped men, women, children jumping, lying down, throwing, sitting, wrestling, carrying, etc. 390pp. 7⅞ × 10⅝.
20204-6 Cloth. $24.95

THE MAN WHO WAS THURSDAY, Gilbert Keith Chesterton. Witty, fast-paced novel about a club of anarchists in turn-of-the-century London. Brilliant social, religious, philosophical speculations. 128pp. 5⅜ × 8½.
25121-7 Pa. $3.95

A CÉZANNE SKETCHBOOK: Figures, Portraits, Landscapes and Still Lifes, Paul Cézanne. Great artist experiments with tonal effects, light, mass, other qualities in over 100 drawings. A revealing view of developing master painter, precursor of Cubism. 102 black-and-white illustrations. 144pp. 8¾ × 6⅝.
24790-2 Pa. $6.95

AN ENCYCLOPEDIA OF BATTLES: Accounts of Over 1,560 Battles from 1479 B.C. to the Present, David Eggenberger. Presents essential details of every major battle in recorded history, from the first battle of Megiddo in 1479 B.C. to Grenada in 1984. List of Battle Maps. New Appendix covering the years 1967–1984. Index. 99 illustrations. 544pp. 6½ × 9¼.
24913-1 Pa. $14.95

AN ETYMOLOGICAL DICTIONARY OF MODERN ENGLISH, Ernest Weekley. Richest, fullest work, by foremost British lexicographer. Detailed word histories. Inexhaustible. Total of 856pp. 6½ × 9¼.
21873-2, 21874-0 Pa., Two-vol. set $19.90

WEBSTER'S AMERICAN MILITARY BIOGRAPHIES, edited by Robert McHenry. Over 1,000 figures who shaped 3 centuries of American military history. Detailed biographies of Nathan Hale, Douglas MacArthur, Mary Hallaren, others. Chronologies of engagements, more. Introduction. Addenda. 1,033 entries in alphabetical order. xi + 548pp. 6½ × 9¼. (Available in U.S. only)
24758-9 Pa. $13.95

LIFE IN ANCIENT EGYPT, Adolf Erman. Detailed older account, with much not in more recent books: domestic life, religion, magic, medicine, commerce, and whatever else needed for complete picture. Many illustrations. 597pp. 5⅜ × 8½.
22632-8 Pa. $9.95

HISTORIC COSTUME IN PICTURES, Braun & Schneider. Over 1,450 costumed figures shown, covering a wide variety of peoples: kings, emperors, nobles, priests, servants, soldiers, scholars, townsfolk, peasants, merchants, courtiers, cavaliers, and more. 256pp. 8⅜ × 11¼.
23150-X Pa. $9.95

THE NOTEBOOKS OF LEONARDO DA VINCI, edited by J. P. Richter. Extracts from manuscripts reveal great genius; on painting, sculpture, anatomy, sciences, geography, etc. Both Italian and English. 186 ms. pages reproduced, plus 500 additional drawings, including studies for *Last Supper, Sforza* monument, etc. 860pp. 7⅞ × 10¾. (Available in U.S. only) 22572-0, 22573-9 Pa., Two-vol. set $35.90

THE ART NOUVEAU STYLE BOOK OF ALPHONSE MUCHA: All 72 Plates from "Documents Decoratifs" in Original Color, Alphonse Mucha. Rare copyright-free design portfolio by high priest of Art Nouveau. Jewelry, wallpaper, stained glass, furniture, figure studies, plant and animal motifs, etc. Only complete one-volume edition. 80pp. 9⅜ × 12¼. 24044-4 Pa. $9.95

ANIMALS: 1,419 COPYRIGHT-FREE ILLUSTRATIONS OF MAMMALS, BIRDS, FISH, INSECTS, ETC., edited by Jim Harter. Clear wood engravings present, in extremely lifelike poses, over 1,000 species of animals. One of the most extensive pictorial sourcebooks of its kind. Captions. Index. 284pp. 9 × 12.
23766-4 Pa. $9.95

OBELISTS FLY HIGH, C. Daly King. Masterpiece of American detective fiction, long out of print, involves murder on a 1935 transcontinental flight—"a very thrilling story"—NY Times. Unabridged and unaltered republication of the edition published by William Collins Sons & Co. Ltd., London, 1935. 288pp. 5⅜ × 8½. (Available in U.S. only) 25036-9 Pa. $5.95

VICTORIAN AND EDWARDIAN FASHION: A Photographic Survey, Alison Gernsheim. First fashion history completely illustrated by contemporary photographs. Full text plus 235 photos, 1840–1914, in which many celebrities appear. 240pp. 6½ × 9¼. 24205-6 Pa. $8.95

THE ART OF THE FRENCH ILLUSTRATED BOOK, 1700–1914, Gordon N. Ray. Over 630 superb book illustrations by Fragonard, Delacroix, Daumier, Doré, Grandville, Manet, Mucha, Steinlen, Toulouse-Lautrec and many others. Preface. Introduction. 633 halftones. Indices of artists, authors & titles, binders and provenances. Appendices. Bibliography. 608pp. 8⅜ × 11¼. 25086-5 Pa. $24.95

THE WONDERFUL WIZARD OF OZ, L. Frank Baum. Facsimile in full color of America's finest children's classic. 143 illustrations by W. W. Denslow. 267pp. 5⅜ × 8½. 20691-2 Pa. $7.95

FOLLOWING THE EQUATOR: A Journey Around the World, Mark Twain. Great writer's 1897 account of circumnavigating the globe by steamship. Ironic humor, keen observations, vivid and fascinating descriptions of exotic places. 197 illustrations. 720pp. 5⅜ × 8½. 26113-1 Pa. $15.95

THE FRIENDLY STARS, Martha Evans Martin & Donald Howard Menzel. Classic text marshalls the stars together in an engaging, non-technical survey, presenting them as sources of beauty in night sky. 23 illustrations. Foreword. 2 star charts. Index. 147pp. 5⅜ × 8½. 21099-5 Pa. $3.95

FADS AND FALLACIES IN THE NAME OF SCIENCE, Martin Gardner. Fair, witty appraisal of cranks, quacks, and quackeries of science and pseudoscience: hollow earth, Velikovsky, orgone energy, Dianetics, flying saucers, Bridey Murphy, food and medical fads, etc. Revised, expanded In the Name of Science. "A very able and even-tempered presentation."—The New Yorker. 363pp. 5⅜ × 8.

20394-8 Pa. $6.95

ANCIENT EGYPT: ITS CULTURE AND HISTORY, J. E Manchip White. From pre-dynastics through Ptolemies: society, history, political structure, religion, daily life, literature, cultural heritage. 48 plates. 217pp. 5⅜ × 8½. 22548-8 Pa. $5.95

SIR HARRY HOTSPUR OF HUMBLETHWAITE, Anthony Trollope. Incisive, unconventional psychological study of a conflict between a wealthy baronet, his idealistic daughter, and their scapegrace cousin. The 1870 novel in its first inexpensive edition in years. 250pp. 5⅜ × 8½.   24953-0 Pa. $6.95

LASERS AND HOLOGRAPHY, Winston E. Kock. Sound introduction to burgeoning field, expanded (1981) for second edition. Wave patterns, coherence, lasers, diffraction, zone plates, properties of holograms, recent advances. 84 illustrations. 160pp. 5⅜ × 8¼. (Except in United Kingdom)   24041-X Pa. $3.95

INTRODUCTION TO ARTIFICIAL INTELLIGENCE: Second, Enlarged Edition, Philip C. Jackson, Jr. Comprehensive survey of artificial intelligence—the study of how machines (computers) can be made to act intelligently. Includes introductory and advanced material. Extensive notes updating the main text. 132 black-and-white illustrations. 512pp. 5⅜ × 8½.   24864-X Pa. $10.95

HISTORY OF INDIAN AND INDONESIAN ART, Ananda K. Coomaraswamy. Over 400 illustrations illuminate classic study of Indian art from earliest Harappa finds to early 20th century. Provides philosophical, religious and social insights. 304pp. 6⅜ × 9⅜.   25005-9 Pa. $11.95

THE GOLEM, Gustav Meyrink. Most famous supernatural novel in modern European literature, set in Ghetto of Old Prague around 1890. Compelling story of mystical experiences, strange transformations, profound terror. 13 black-and-white illustrations. 224pp. 5⅜ × 8½. (Available in U.S. only)   25025-3 Pa. $6.95

PICTORIAL ENCYCLOPEDIA OF HISTORIC ARCHITECTURAL PLANS, DETAILS AND ELEMENTS: With 1,880 Line Drawings of Arches, Domes, Doorways, Facades, Gables, Windows, etc., John Theodore Haneman. Sourcebook of inspiration for architects, designers, others. Bibliography. Captions. 141pp. 9 × 12.
                                                              24605-1 Pa. $8.95

BENCHLEY LOST AND FOUND, Robert Benchley. Finest humor from early 30s, about pet peeves, child psychologists, post office and others. Mostly unavailable elsewhere. 73 illustrations by Peter Arno and others. 183pp. 5⅜ × 8½.
                                                              22410-4 Pa. $4.95

ERTÉ GRAPHICS, Erté. Collection of striking color graphics: *Seasons, Alphabet, Numerals, Aces* and *Precious Stones.* 50 plates, including 4 on covers. 48pp. 9⅜ × 12¼.
                                                              23580-7 Pa. $7.95

THE JOURNAL OF HENRY D. THOREAU, edited by Bradford Torrey, F. H. Allen. Complete reprinting of 14 volumes, 1837–61, over two million words; the sourcebooks for *Walden,* etc. Definitive. All original sketches, plus 75 photographs. 1,804pp. 8½ × 12¼.   20312-3, 20313-1 Cloth., Two-vol. set $130.00

CASTLES: Their Construction and History, Sidney Toy. Traces castle development from ancient roots. Nearly 200 photographs and drawings illustrate moats, keeps, baileys, many other features. Caernarvon, Dover Castles, Hadrian's Wall, Tower of London, dozens more. 256pp. 5⅜ × 8¼.   24898-4 Pa. $7.95

AMERICAN CLIPPER SHIPS: 1833–1858, Octavius T. Howe & Frederick C. Matthews. Fully-illustrated, encyclopedic review of 352 clipper ships from the period of America's greatest maritime supremacy. Introduction. 109 halftones. 5 black-and-white line illustrations. Index. Total of 928pp. 5⅜ × 8½.
25115-2, 25116-0 Pa., Two-vol. set $17.90

TOWARDS A NEW ARCHITECTURE, Le Corbusier. Pioneering manifesto by great architect, near legendary founder of "International School." Technical and aesthetic theories, views on industry, economics, relation of form to function, "mass-production spirit," much more. Profusely illustrated. Unabridged translation of 13th French edition. Introduction by Frederick Etchells. 320pp. 6⅛ × 9¼. (Available in U.S. only)
25023-7 Pa. $8.95

THE BOOK OF KELLS, edited by Blanche Cirker. Inexpensive collection of 32 full-color, full-page plates from the greatest illuminated manuscript of the Middle Ages, painstakingly reproduced from rare facsimile edition. Publisher's Note. Captions. 32pp. 9⅜ × 12¼. (Available in U.S. only)
24345-1 Pa. $5.95

BEST SCIENCE FICTION STORIES OF H. G. WELLS, H. G. Wells. Full novel *The Invisible Man,* plus 17 short stories: "The Crystal Egg," "Aepyornis Island," "The Strange Orchid," etc. 303pp. 5⅜ × 8½. (Available in U.S. only)
21531-8 Pa. $6.95

AMERICAN SAILING SHIPS: Their Plans and History, Charles G. Davis. Photos, construction details of schooners, frigates, clippers, other sailcraft of 18th to early 20th centuries—plus entertaining discourse on design, rigging, nautical lore, much more. 137 black-and-white illustrations. 240pp. 6⅛ × 9¼.
24658-2 Pa. $6.95

ENTERTAINING MATHEMATICAL PUZZLES, Martin Gardner. Selection of author's favorite conundrums involving arithmetic, money, speed, etc., with lively commentary. Complete solutions. 112pp. 5⅜ × 8½.
25211-6 Pa. $3.50

THE WILL TO BELIEVE, HUMAN IMMORTALITY, William James. Two books bound together. Effect of irrational on logical, and arguments for human immortality. 402pp. 5⅜ × 8½.
20291-7 Pa. $8.95

THE HAUNTED MONASTERY and THE CHINESE MAZE MURDERS, Robert Van Gulik. 2 full novels by Van Gulik continue adventures of Judge Dee and his companions. An evil Taoist monastery, seemingly supernatural events; overgrown topiary maze that hides strange crimes. Set in 7th-century China. 27 illustrations. 328pp. 5⅜ × 8½.
23502-5 Pa. $6.95

CELEBRATED CASES OF JUDGE DEE (DEE GOONG AN), translated by Robert Van Gulik. Authentic 18th-century Chinese detective novel; Dee and associates solve three interlocked cases. Led to Van Gulik's own stories with same characters. Extensive introduction. 9 illustrations. 237pp. 5⅜ × 8½.
23337-5 Pa. $5.95

Prices subject to change without notice.

Available at your book dealer or write for free catalog to Dept. GI, Dover Publications, Inc., 31 East 2nd St., Mineola, N.Y. 11501. Dover publishes more than 175 books each year on science, elementary and advanced mathematics, biology, music, art, literary history, social sciences and other areas.